OTHERWISE FINE

OTHERWISE FINE

*Moving Outside the Frame
to
Conquer the Fears of Dying*

Susan Barry

C. B. ROMILLY BOOKS
Austin, Texas

OTHERWISE FINE

Copyright © 2005 by Susan Barry

C. B. Romilly Books
Austin, Texas

All rights reserved.
No part of this book may be reproduced or utilized in any form or
by any means, electronic or mechanical, including photocopying,
recording or by any information storage and retrieval system
without permission in writing.

First Printing 2005
Second Printing 2005

Cataloguing-in-Publication Data

Barry, Susan
Otherwise Fine: Moving Outside the Frame to Conquer the Fears of Dying
    p.   cm.   index

1. Death–Spiritual aspects. 2. Death–Social aspects. 3. Eschatology–Fears.
4. Spiritual life. 5. Future life. 6. Death–Psychology: anxiety.
I. Title. II. Author. III. Monograph

ISBN 0-97637770-5 pbk

BF 789 D4 B   155.937 Ba   2004099101

> Although information herein is based on the author's extensive
> experience and knowledge, it is not intended to substitute for the
> services of qualified professionals.

Illustration: Rebecca Byrd Bretz
Cover design: Stephen Bright
Author photo: Beth Van Houten

Printed in the United States of America
at Morgan Printing in Austin, Texas

DEDICATED

above all, to Brice and Drew

gratefully, to Drew and Rick,
for their early affirmation and encouragement

to the memory of Dee and Paupau,
who gifted me with unconditional love

to Mike, who supported me
during the second vile period in my life

to my beloved, enduring friends around the country

*A*CKNOWLEDGING

in order of their appearance on the journey

The esteemed Robert J. Kastenbaum for his high standards, generosity of time and personal warmth; the remarkable Edwin Shneidman; the catalytic trio of Robert E. Kavanaugh, now deceased, Lisl Goodman and Robert Jay Lifton; and their peers in the field of death education, whose contributions and career excellence are sampled in these pages.

As well as Philip Simmons, now deceased; Davidson Loehr; and Ernest Noble.

With equal gratitude to
Karen Armstrong and Anne Primavesi,
whom I met late in my research and
whose works clarified and enriched the book.

And Patricia Saunders, my delightful and gifted editor, whose accomplished technical skills and creative hands carried these pages from editing to indexing.

Contents

Preface A Dazzling Journey 1

Part I
Loss of the Self

The fears of unmet potentials and extinction with insignificance 11

Chapter 1 The Fear of Incompleteness 15

Chapter 2 The Post-Self 32
    Getting Personal with Lifton's Modes 36
    Gertrude 42

Chapter 3 The Real Self
    Late- and Never-Bloomers 45
    Extra Steps for Two Profiles 48

Chapter 4 Prescriptions 55
    Meaning and Purpose in Life 62

Chapter 5 Moving Outside the Frame 73

Part II
Loss of the Physical Self

The fears of pain, dependency and the loss of control 83

Chapter 6 Let Go and Let WHO? 85

Chapter 7 Coping
    A Personal Role Model 95

Forecasting the Weather 99
...and Dressing for It 105

Chapter 8 The Needs of the Dying 114
The Main Four 119

PART III
WHAT THEN?

*The fears of nothingness, judgment and
the unknown* 131

Chapter 9 The Cons of an Afterlife Belief 133

Chapter 10 The Pros of an Afterlife Belief 150
The Death of Ellen Augusta 151
Psychic Phenomena: A Bottom Line 157

Chapter 11 All Things Considered 176
Spirituality and Faith 178

AFTERWORDS 191
Two Women and a Boat 193

BIBLIOGRAPHY 199

INDEX 209

ABOUT THE AUTHOR 223

Preface

A Dazzling Journey

When I was five, I had an unforgettable dream. I was running after my beloved and highly accomplished grandfather. He stepped into an elevator and turned around to face me. The elevator went up. I went tumbling down its black shaft. Such childhood dreams often foretell the myth of a life.

Since I grab at any moment or event that sniffs of symbol, I take rainbows personally and used to dread those metaphoric messages that came through at night. Suddenly, in my forties, the signals changed, beginning with a gloriously bucolic dream filled with green meadows and—I swear—sheep. The next night I soared effortlessly over Grand Canyon.

So it was the dream pattern changed and has remained since the day I was sitting in a university library and realized I had overcome my fear of death. Those dreams, bearing peace, celebrated that victory and verified the banishment of some ugly demons. Initially, I had recorded on paper the insights into dying that I had found in my research, to give to family and friends.

Then my son Drew encouraged me to expand.
But for whom?

Those from early to later middle age when death anxiety peaks, those entering a terminal illness, those supporting them—all are clearly beneficiaries.

There are also those with specific profiles who may be especially helped by information that has become Part I of this book: those with low self-esteem, those with little or no luck at critical junctures, those who come from dysfunctional childhood environments, those who as children have not received parental mirroring of the needs of their developing personalities.

Also, having written an article—"Alcoholics and Death Anxiety"—for a professional publication,[1] I knew the healing that this research could bring to those in recovery from addictions, regardless of the substance.

In surveys sorted by gender, women indicate a greater propensity for high levels of anxiety. Further, death anxiety is heightened in many for whom work is a means to an end, rather than an end in itself, as it is for many quasi-believers, who fall somewhere between being confirmed atheists and devout "good theology" believers.

Especially surprising were responses to my own random sampling. I mentioned an optional subtitle, "Overcoming 'Blew It' Anxiety and Other Fears of Dying," to some highly accomplished friends whose pasts fit none of these profiles. Enviously, I would classify them as over-achieving personal and professional successes. Yet, their eyes lit up in recognition of and with an appetite for the subject. Go figure!

Human examples and certain themes common to almost all spiritual traditions occasionally fit as complementary punctuation to consensus opinions of the secular death educators. I incorporated both where appropriate. The resulting first draft, an impersonally dry, academic precursor to this book, I gave to a leading thanatologist for his opinion.

Robert J. Kastenbaum's many credits include professor

emeritus at Arizona State University, editor-in-chief of *Omega: Journal of Death and Dying*, prolific author in the field of death education, and a founding light of The Association for Death Education and Counseling. "What I would like to see," Dr. Kastenbaum said, "is for you to react and enter the text in a personal way."

Appreciative of his advice, I changed the direction and tone of my book. It shifted into an introduction to me as well as to my research adventure. My voice and the expert insights have fallen together in a straight line, like numbers on a winning Bingo card.

Who, being in good health and humor and in possession of a Mercedes, would voluntarily leave the sunshine of Santa Barbara to hunker down in university libraries seeking relief for her death anxiety?

I would. And how I came to take that life-making journey will appear where relevant to the text. Certainly, included in that early childhood dream were the expectations of a family. Foretold in it, too, was a devastating divorce that would affect me and two small, wonderful children. Along the way, I gained some hefty insights.

If you have not learned and maintained boundaries in defense of your self-esteem, you will be that vulnerable sitting duck and ugly to yourself. If someone—who later rejects you—likes or even loves you for your true self, the wound may even be cancerous; you lack immunity. But if you carry around the banner of the walking wounded as an excuse to atrophy, you deserve the oblivion. On this I was a quick learner.

Then came more significant insights, not my own but ones found at the end of a research journey that changed my life and became this book. Significantly, I uncovered them by following yet another foretelling Myth Indicator we each are given in childhood. It is one that Joseph Campbell knew well.

Recall what it was that you did as a child in which you lost all sense of time passing. Therein lies your rightful life myth.[2] It is your own unique myth that lies beyond the control of parental programming and circumstance, and the one with all the clues to your happiness. You can count on it always to give you fulfillment and direction.

I thought back to those activities I did as a child during which I blissfully lost track of time. The one that stood out was reading. When I was older, it was researching in a library those topics which intrigued me. So it was mythically correct that one of those freelance, $8-an-hour jobs at which I jumped held opportunity for both intellectual challenge and my passions for books and library research. As a cataloguer at a rare-book house, I was hired to help get out the next catalogue edition of current offerings. I knew squat about cataloguing. Perhaps I was hired because the owner was a bit infatuated with me, albeit not enough to extend the job offer beyond the 1099 level and pay my social security taxes.

A word about cataloguing. You take a first edition, manuscript, illuminated page, letter, photograph or, if allowed, a piece of incunabula, books predating 1501. Your job has two components.

First is to tell what the subject is and why it is valuable. This points to the importance of the author and/or subject and the more important consideration of supply and demand.

The second is to write up the condition of the item, which involves using a precious vocabulary all its own. *Recto* and *verso* for right- and left-hand page sides of an open book; *octavo*, *quarto* and *folio* for item sizes; and a circus of abbreviations like A.L. for Autograph or handwritten Letter and A.L.s for Autograph Letter, signed.

Throw in words like *niger, sheep, yapp yapp, wrappers, stubbed, states, yellow backs,* and *deckle-fetishism,* and you begin to have fun. Disclaiming warnings of condition such as *shaky, loose, foxed* and *limp*, ubiquitously and humorously you conclude with *else fine* or *otherwise fine.*

The research resources required for the item's content analysis and promotion come generally, but not always exclusively, from two exhilarating sets of encyclopedias. *The Dictionary of National Biography* (DNB) includes authors and works related to Great Britain. *The Dictionary of American Biography* (DAB) includes our own respected authors and works. The DNB and DAB are the most frequent sources cited in your write-up, and the many volumes of each are usually within steps of your desk. To enter their world is like getting a Ph.D. in English and history and never wanting to graduate from the spellbinding tales these volumes hold.

Thus, it was natural to the synchronicity of this moment in my life that I drove one day to the huge University of California Library nearby to research my fear of dying. The baggage I took may have been uniquely my own, but the quest was not, nor most certainly were the answers I found.

My fear was not the panic variety, but it was indeed the kind that brought butterflies at the sign of trouble swallowing or a breast lump. It was the looking-down-the-road specter with which I had not made peace.

The philosopher often called America's first psychologist, William James dubbed this universal fear "the worm at the core." Many argue it caused the birth of gods and salvation religions, a terror the animal kingdom is blissfully spared.

We humans, though, are not spared. A fair statement of many adult conditions could be: Some chipping and foxing affecting text, heavy wear to cover, spine loose, insidious worm inside, otherwise fine.

The Hindus have a saying, *kicking the frame.* It means "to die." Another frame metaphor comes to mind, the one of which Oliver Wendell Holmes spoke: "To live greatly one must disregard the limit and have his picture end like a Japanese drawing, *outside the frame.*"³

What can be a better goal than to find now the opening that will ultimately take you across and outside of this earthly frame? Surely if such a bridge can be found, it will bring you all the inner peace you will need to face the dying stage itself.

I never bought the Old Man in the Sky as the only viable lighthouse for such a crossing, or even the best one. So, it was really a search for that opening in the frame that sent me off for hours, then years to sit cross-legged on the floors of academic libraries, from the University of California to the British Museum's august Reading Room in London, combing primarily the philosophy, psychology and sociology sections.

One of the by-products of confronting the "worm" is the resulting emotional ease that can serve others through their final days. As a volunteer in my twenties, I was a cancer program coordinator. Deep down, I was anchored in a get-well mode, protectively blinkered from the alternative.

Minus this research experience, I never could have been comfortable as a hospice team member decades later, as indeed I have been in both a volunteer and professional capacity. Although my time with terminal patients and the bereaved is separate and private, it sanctions this solid affirmation. It has been infinitely gratifying to go from the wisdom of many past centuries to its uniquely individualized, living examples and see that, definitely, it all does hold as one piece.

I especially hope the substance has value for those who by circumstance or choice know they will face the dying stage without significant others, apart from medical staff, to support them. My concern also is for whoever feels a need to have left some small but worthwhile mark. Unabashedly, however, I begin with my own malaise. How many share and suffer 'Blew It' Death Anxiety? It matters zero if others would agree with such self-assessment. It matters only how we feel about ourselves in a clutch, looking down the road.

Of the books cited, few will be found in neighborhood bookstores or the smaller public libraries, as so many colors in the field of death education are not. Most, if not all, are now available through Internet booksellers; you can recognize the scholarly, academic ones by their prices! Many of these books and the papers collected in medical journals and periodicals have been written by clinical researchers, teaching doctors and university scholars.

What had I read that was so extraordinary, so *dazzling* in the true sense of that word?

To start with, a familiar truth: Learning about dying is learning about living. There is no better time to acquit suppressed dread than in our prime, the early and middle years when death anxiety peaks. As the popular Joseph Campbell promised, "The conquest of the fear of death is the recovery of life's joy."[4] As the academic Robert E. Kavanaugh put it as conclusion to his book *Facing Death*, "Never have I enjoyed life more, dreamed more beautiful dreams each night, than when I began having courage to begin facing death."[5]

So, too, was my experience. Those idyllic dreams during and after research were transformational metaphors. I go back and revisit the core insights, which are ageless, whenever I feel myself drifting into daily turmoil or health fears. The big picture is beautiful, but it is easily lost in the woods.

Thanatologists and U.S. surveys cited address death attitudes and truths as they reflect Western, not Eastern, cultures except where commonality is noted. To focus on the key leitmotifs I found repeated time and again, I do not digress into death fears of and for children and unrelated end-of-life issues like euthanasia.

For structuring purposes, the material is divided into three parts. First addressed are the psychological fears of an inauthentic life and extinction with insignificance, then the fears involving the physical process itself, and finally the fears of separation, nothingness, judgment and the unknown after the bodily death. The most relief for my personal death anxiety, which may be the fear least addressed in popular print, I found in researching the first part of this book: the life-transforming possibility of death education.

The second part is intended to be a hands-on rudder, either for navigating an individual course or for being a helpmate to a loved one during the final stage of physically letting go.

The last part focuses on the pros and cons of belief in an afterlife. I have excluded all popular bestseller and television personality names in psychic phenomena in favor of material which is either fact or which has undergone rigorous scrutiny but is rarely cited and known by the general public.

The elusive nature of certain areas is best exemplified by my frustration in tracking down support for a relationship between lowered death anxiety and a belief in an afterlife. No reliable, polled statistics are on tap. As both a hospice minister and a nursing therapist with the terminally ill pointed out, the other side of the religious coin from the happy hunting ground is the wrathful "bad theology" programming which can heighten anxiety in believers.

My quest for a majority Western consensus was defeated finally by the realization that such studies were vulnerable. For example, a low anxiety score could mean high denial. Kastenbaum confirms that people who lack a sense of security and effective self-mastery tend to report greater levels of death anxiety and, indeed, notes the function of past and future regrets as another measure. Available research still cannot clarify conclusively the relationship between religiosity and death anxiety.[6]

In short, accuracy in polled percentages of attitudes

towards death and dying has been doomed because *there are so many variables*. Kastenbaum makes the insightful observation that perhaps the real variable is whether or not there is a life-threatening situation present to activate the death anxiety. At other risk-free times, without any precipitating arousal, the terror remains dormant. In these periods there is normal low-to-moderate anxiety. We are not in "denial;" we are simply not at risk, Kastenbaum suggests. He observes some findings do merit attention, among them, that women admit to a higher death anxiety level than men.[7] Most definitely, the consensus is that lower death anxiety is associated with having a purpose in life and/or high self-esteem and also with the feeling of being in control of your life.

Now deceased, Ernest Becker wrote these words in 1973 in his Pulitzer Prize-winning *The Denial of Death* and just as easily might write them today: "The problem is how to make sense of it; the accumulation of research and opinion on the fear of death is already too large to be dealt with and summarized in any simple way. The revival of interest in death in the last few decades has alone piled up a formidable literature, and this literature does not point in any single direction."[8]

I'm not so sure.

Despite the centuries of complex material from academia, world religions and science, *a few clear signals keep reappearing in the same directions*. If there is no quick fix out there for the psychological fear of death, it turns out there is still one very real directive we can follow to transcend it. Moreover, there are four solid guideposts on how to ride out the dying stage, and intriguing material exists on what may lie beyond it.

[1] Barry, Susan. "Alcoholics and Death Anxiety." *The Forum: A Publication of the Association for Death Education and Counseling.* West Hartford, CT: Lebon Press Inc. 17.2 (1992): 8.
[2] Osbon, Diane K., ed. *A Joseph Campbell Companion: Reflections on the Art of Living.* New York: Harper-Collins, 1991, p. 181.
[3] Holmes, Oliver Wendell, Jr. *Holmes-Einstein Letters.* (1910). London: Macmillan, 1964, p. 56.
[4] Campbell, Joseph, with Bill Moyers. *The Power of Myth.* 3rd Ed. Betty Sue Flowers, ed. New York: Doubleday, 1988, p. 152.
[5] Kavanaugh, Robert E. *Facing Death.* Los Angeles: Nash, 1972, p. 226.
[6] Kastenbaum, Robert J., Ph.D. *Death, Society, and Human Experience.* 8th Ed. Boston: Allyn & Bacon, 2003, pp. 32-43.
[7] —. *The Psychology of Death.* 3rd Ed. New York: Springer, 2000, pp. 119-21, 152-56.
[8] Becker, Ernest, Dr. *The Denial of Death.* New York: Free Press, 1973, pp. 12-13.

PART I

LOSS OF THE SELF

The fears of unmet potentials and extinction with insignificance

From Jeremy Taylor's Renaissance bestseller *The Rule and Exercises of Holy Dying* (1651), "The Epistle Dedicatory":

> *My Lord, it is a great art to dye well, and to be learnt by men in health....He who prepares not for death, before his last sicknesse, is like him that begins to study Philosophy when he is going to dispute publikely in the faculty...and therefore (my Lord) it is intended by the necessity of affairs, that the precepts of dying well be part of the studies of them that live in health...for we die but once; and therefore it will be necessary that our skill be more exact, since it is not to be mended by triall.*[1]

From French essayist Michel de Montaigne (1533-92), *To Learn How to Die*. No one has said it better than this:

> Let us learn to meet (death) steadfastly and to combat it....Let us rid it of its strangeness, come to know it; get used to it. **Premeditation of death is premeditation of freedom. He who has learned how to die has unlearned how to be a slave**....He who would teach men to die would teach them to live....**The constant work of your life is to build death.**

From Nathan Scott's *The Modern Vision of Death* (1967), describing the conviction of German philosopher and thanatologist Martin Heidegger, one which essentially expresses a general consensus among resources:

> It is only by unblinkingly facing his eventual annulment that a man can be delivered from the trivializing cares of the normal daily round and enabled to dedicate himself to projects where his human career may be given some really high significance.

From Ernest Becker's Pulitzer Prize-winning *The Denial of Death* (1973), referring to William James' colorful metaphor for the terror of death:

> [Although] repression takes care of the complex symbol of death for most people, [the terror remains] "the worm at the core" of man's pretensions to happiness.

From Rabbi Krauss in *Why Me? Coping with Death, Loss and Change* (1988), the one about

> *...the atheist mountain climber who lost his grip as he approached the summit but managed to grab a branch that stopped his fall.*
>
> *Holding on for dear life, he called out, "God, You haven't been part of my life, and I didn't even think You existed. But I need help now. Please, God! If You can help me, I'll be Your follower. Answer me if You are there!"*
>
> *Suddenly a loud and clear voice responded, "My son, I know you haven't been faithful, but here I am. Do you trust Me?"*
>
> *The man answered, "Oh yes, I do now."*
>
> *The voice continued, "Then trust in Me and let go."*
>
> *There was a pause.*
>
> *"Is there anyone else up there?" the man shouted.*

**PART I is about
confronting death, overcoming fears and letting go.**

CHAPTER 1

THE FEAR OF INCOMPLETENESS

entelechy n. 1. In the philosophy of Aristotle, the condition of a thing whose essence is fully realized; actuality as distinguished from potentiality. 2. In various philosophical systems, a vital force urging an organism toward self-fulfillment.[2]

"I don't think people are afraid of death. What they are afraid of is the incompleteness of their life." With these words of Ted Rosenthal, who at the age of 30 learned that he was dying of leukemia, clinical psychologist Lisl Goodman begins *Death and the Creative Life*.[3]

Had Rosenthal said the regret or even anger of an incomplete life, he would have meant the understandable reaction to an untimely death early in life. But he designates *fear*. Therefore, does he not mean by "an incomplete life" a life whose potential and goals have not yet been fully realized?

And which ones? Of roads outside the safety net that beckoned and were never traveled? Or calls to bliss never followed along creative and exotic detours that would have brought fulfilling pleasure? Or the call never heeded to follow your aptitude, revealed by that SAT math score, that would have given you no pleasure but fame and conceivably a Nobel Prize? Or special relationships not nurtured?

Or does the fear of incompleteness mean simply the desperate angst of believing you've blown it in and with your life? Whether at 30 or 70, time can and does run out.

Along with the fear of unmet potentials comes the existential fear of death that is the fear of non-existence or annihilation. These and their associated fears of separation, judgment and the unknown are distinguishable from the fears of dependency, pain and loss of control. The latter fears have to do with the process of dying and are likely easier to assuage.

Part II will address this second group. However, these two groups of fears are a hand-in-glove team. By applying them to life now, not only does the quality of *your* eventual dying change, but also that of those whom you may support in *theirs*.

Many books have been written on the gifts parents can but often do not bestow on their children—feelings of security, self-esteem, values, unconditional love. Conversely, there may be no greater gift a child can give a parent or a friend can give a dying friend than to integrate and resolve these specific fears now rather than having to work through them then.

My first focus is the death anxiety attributable to unrealized potentials. This is not everyone's primary fear. However, because of America's excessive investment in individualism, there may be a surprisingly large number in this country afflicted by its downside relative to the loss of self. In my opinion, the challenge American individualism, uniquely virulent even among Western cultures, presents to death anxiety is the most profound issue in my research. From this viewpoint on philosophical and psychological fears of death, here is Dr. Goodman's development of three concepts:

1. Fear of death is primarily fear of dying prematurely, before we have actualized our potentials.
2. Full acknowledgement of our finiteness intensifies our awareness of life, of the limited amount of time at our disposal and, as a galvanizing force, propels us toward realization of our talents or desires.
3. If we succeed in giving form to the unique possibilities within ourselves, we experience self-fulfillment. At this point, life is completed and the death can truly be called a natural one.

"The experience of self-fulfillment may not lie in actually reaching the ultimate goal, but in the satisfaction and success of the hunt....Put in the simplest form, the more one is 'doing one's own thing,' the more one feels satisfied with life—and, by implication, can better deal with the prospect of death." [4]

To both Goodman and Rosenthal "completeness" means self-actualization, and the term *self* refers to the *authentic* self. I stress this because I gave the phrase "the fear of incompleteness" to two quite intelligent friends. Both immediately interpreted it to mean *the angst of leading or having led an **inauthentic** life*. For Goodman, *dying prematurely is dying before one's psychological needs are met. Unrealized potentials and an inauthentic life are the consequence of not meeting one's psychological needs.*

The distinction needs to be clear between psychological needs and aptitude. When Joseph Campbell gave us the rallying cry, "Follow your Bliss!" he did not mean to follow your SAT math score of 800 into careers in engineering or astrophysics unless your passion and bliss, the very hallmarks of your authenticity, were there also. (By example, academically my own math aptitude is my highest, but I would prefer the Chinese water torture to a life of equations in any guise).

The obvious solution, then, to determining individual potentials and goals is to pinpoint where psychological needs and aptitude intersect and to integrate them as well as possible when making career and relationship choices. Opportunities for realizing many other potentials of the authentic self extend to every nook of our waking hours and to every defining sentence we speak.

In the end, it is about getting and staying kinetic, running with the right ball instead of dropping it on the sidelines and taking a nap. The biggest hitch is recognizing and catching the right ball in the first place. And in the real world, it rarely is the one available *in the first place,* is it?

Karen Armstrong went into a convent at age seventeen on a blissful quest of union with God. She emerged seven years later, a failure at prayer, at any relationship with God or even with herself, from whom she could no longer elicit one original idea. With temporal lobe epilepsy (undiagnosed until 1976), she went on to anorexia, a brush with suicide, frozen emotions and the inability to express or feel love even for her family. Failing to earn her Ph.D. at Oxford was followed by failing unceremoniously at a television career.

Once, the calling to bliss she had followed. Now, the very thought of God tired her. This is not a tale of being drawn from childhood into a magnetic field toward the authentic meaning for her life, is it? Someone gave Armstrong a bad date with Destiny, if so.

Before the television doors closed on her, however, Armstrong had worked successfully on a television series about religion. She laughs about her horrified reaction to the plum, on-air reporting assignment that put her back in the religious soup. On location in Jerusalem she met the richness of Judaism and Islam, faiths which had been strangers to her. Enthralled, she told publishers her idea of writing *A History of God*.

"Not '*re-lee-gion*'," they moaned. "A travel book or biography. Anything but religion. Anything but God."

She alone felt the spark and drive towards this subject. Consequently, in the face of predictions of more doom and failure, she took the risk. Armstrong related this story in 2004 during a presentation about her autobiography just published. In promotional copy for that book, *The Spiral Staircase*, her fellow colleague and esteemed author Marcus Borg called her "contemporary religion's foremost public intellectual." Carolyn See wrote in the *Washington Post*, "I'm honored to be reviewing this book....It is a story about becoming human, being recognized, finally recognizing oneself....*More than anything, it fills the reader with hope.*"

She stands in front of her audience, devoid of pretension, filled with humor, warmth, British wit. Armstrong mentions a recent focus of hers, the sages of the Axial Age of approximately 800-200 B.C., including Confucius, Lao-Tzu, the Buddha and Socrates. She notes they all insisted that one not follow the directions given by others, but determine for oneself what is the right path. She concluded a line in T. S. Eliot's *Ash Wednesday*, "Desiring this man's gift and that man's scope," with a line of her own: "not finding what's right for you."

Karen Armstrong failed in her quest to find God in a nun's prayers and meditation attempts. Years later, to her shock and wonder, she succeeded in finding her bliss in the study of theology. Unable to meditate on the cross, a new, authentic level of consciousness and the outlet she created for it brought her to her passion today: reading, writing and talking about God. Silently reading religious texts, she experienced those moments of transcendence and awe which had once eluded her and whose source now she feels no need to name.

Another person's bliss, she points out, might be a relationship, raising a family, a journey in politics, medicine, poetry or whatever. But it will be what the person loves and will blossom from an authentic core.

In addition to being a beautiful story about realizing authentic potentials, Armstrong's personal odyssey contributes two further messages to the subject here.

The title *The Spiral Staircase* was inspired by Eliot's *Ash Wednesday*, a group of six poems which chronicle the journey of spiritual recovery. The image of the poet in pain is reflected in the repeated phrases and words falling back on themselves and seeming to make scant or no headway. The tortuous sentences go round and around, yet somehow manage to inch ahead steadily, gathering illumination. Just so, Armstrong says, has her own life progressed. Ash Wednesday is a reminder of our mortality, after which we reflect and do penance for a long period which leads to the "rebirth of Easter—a life we could not possibly have imagined at the outset."

Hers seemed a difficult Lenten passage without any hope of an Easter. "I toiled round and round in pointless circles, covering the same ground, repeating the same mistakes, quite unable to see where I was going. Yet all the time, without realizing it, I was slowly climbing out of the darkness." Armstrong notes stairs often symbolized a transforming breakthrough in mythology.[5] How many people have taken this journey and despaired of failure, unable to see the transformative change of consciousness in progress?

The second message comes from a woman in the audience who praised Armstrong's complete lack of phoniness. She observed that it was obvious that Armstrong's *journey was not about her, but something bigger*—and it was *that transcending expansion beyond oneself* that Campbell *called bliss*. She ended, to much agreeing applause, by saying if that bliss can be so apparent in Armstrong, then she knows it must be in her as well.[6] "Expansion beyond one's self" will take shape and direction in the coming pages as death educators focus on the fears of dying and death.

If, like Armstrong, we connect with the right ball to run with, there still will be times our authentic selves are tested. There are choices and watershed events when we are called on to take a stand. These are the moments that define us when, if we are fortunate, the choice becomes an instinctive response and we can join with Martin Luther and say, *"Ich kann nichts anders."* (I can do no other.)

On the rare occasions when those words are felt, be it figuratively or literally before a firing squad for one's beliefs or actions, the fear of death is transcended. If one can look back over a life's course and know, that, on the whole, he or she could do no other, the battle with death anxiety has scored a victory and inner peace is the gain.

Realistically, a person can never lead a completely authentic life, much less fulfill all its potentials. Edwin Shneidman was on target when he wrote, "The cold fact is that most people die too soon or too late, with loose threads and fragments of life's agenda uncompleted."[7] It is an impossible trick to have the natural deaths of both the material and immaterial natures of our existence wind down together. Whether it's war or drunk driving, cancer or the cancer of anger, procrastination or hedonistic human nature, ideal never meets reality. A natural death where rhythms of both body and soul close down together is unlikely. However, it is for the goal of getting as close as possible to this ideal that the following exercises serve.

Regarding mental exercises: The Negative Golden Rule states, "Do not do to others what you would not want others to do to you." I recoil at workshop leaders who hand out pencils for making lists and finally realized my mistake was in signing up for anything with *Goals* in its title. Duh.

This said, your option is to skim or skip the following exercises or to let them change the quality of the rest of your life. The option is also to do a major plumbing job by working through them all or by working only the more comprehensive Simonton or Goodman one.

D-DAYS. The objective of Goodman's exercise is to bring the finish lines of bodily functions and actualized potentials more into alignment by setting Death, or Completion, Days. By so doing, we literally number our days and shape a timetable for fulfillment. This is all about the broad spectrum of unfinished business and getting it done. Of course, after reaching the target date, you continue. Some parts will definitely remain undone, but much more of your best and secret self will have been applied, sustained and healed.

By starting at the best finish line you can think of for yourself, you can decide what lifestyle and choices will get you there. A benefit to the D-Day exercise is seeing a uniquely styled and realized *whole*, a completion (or "completeness" as Rosenthal coined it), whose end point will bear the imprint of your best self-image. Because I find the timetable concept a powerful framework, I prefer this exercise to other guided visualization fantasies that produce the same points.

LIFE REVIEW. Dr. Robert Butler is credited with originating the Life Review process in the early '60s. He described the review as "characterized by the progressive return to consciousness of past experiences and particularly the resurgence of unresolved conflicts that can be looked at again and reintegrated. If the reintegration is successful, it can give new significance and meaning to one's life." [8]

In Ingmar Bergman's film, *Wild Strawberries*, when confronted with the specter of death, the old doctor is obsessed with understanding the meaning of life. The film is a classic study of life-review therapy in regard to that search and may be the best film ever made on the fear of death.

DEATH AND REBIRTH. Carl Simonton and Stephanie Matthews-Simonton popularized Butler's concept in *Getting Well Again*, their celebrated classic. Their step process clarifies attainable goals, helps slough off bad habits and feelings, and inspires new responses and attitudes. Essentially, it is an exercise in death and rebirth.

Beginning with a terminal diagnosis, you let yourself feel your emotional reactions and deteriorating body and the presence, words and emotions of those gathered around your bed. Moving to and through the moment of death and to the service later, you experience the people there, your lifeless body and your consciousness, wherever you sense it will be at that time.

The next step is the reason this exercise has received high marks. The directive is to assess what was good, what you would wish changed and what resentments yet remain. The

exponentially therapeutic result is the awareness that
- *there is yet time to make those changes*
- *the process of death and rebirth is ongoing within each life*
- *changes can occur by simply altering one's beliefs or attitudes*

Of significant note is the fact that it was for cancer patients in the Simontons' clinic that the exercise was originally intended. What I find striking is the unambiguous message that even in what could be the terminal stage, getting it *right* is doable. To quote Confucius, "He who sees the Way in the morning can gladly die in the evening."

There is a classic literary prototype for the person who initially tries desperately to mentally separate himself from one who dies. Tolstoy's simple and ordinary Ivan Illych had never truly felt human kindness and caring until his final days. He experienced a spiritual conversion and came back with compassion for his family and was no longer afraid of death.

Only two hours before he died, he realized a life lived wrong could still be righted. And it was enough. What is significant is not that it was a religious makeover, but rather that it brought the new feeling of being saved into life's final countdown. "Saved" is the operative word here and has everything to do with how we feel about ourselves, not what any god or human community feels and judges about us.

I suggest we who quake in self-recriminations have a task: to accept that it is never too late for the death and rebirth of our self-image and esteem. In our Western culture, it is the job of old-time religion and new-age spiritual grounding to help us accept this affirmation. I believe some of us active spiritual trekkers still carry a hole inside us. Inside the hole, stuffed away and repressed, our unmet potentials and self-indictments lurk. They lurk almost, but not quite, hidden until the first terminal diagnosis is delivered.

The anxiety of that moment brings me back to the words of Ted Rosenthal: "I don't think people are afraid of dying. What they are afraid of is the incompleteness of their life." In Rosenthal's case, untimely early death, not lassitude, prevented the full extent of self-realization.

The other application of "incomplete" is to those with late-life regrets and feelings of having blown it. Both interpretations, though, refer to the regrets of unmet potentials. While I have seen no studies which address this, surely the late-life group feels far more responsibility and guilt than the Rosenthal group, who might justifiably experience the *anger of incompleteness* instead.

Goodman's Death Day exercise reaches out to both these early and late lifers, whether or not a terminal stage has been thrust on them. The Simontons' visualization is like an open invitation to drop by and lacks the urgency and ignition provided by Goodman's timetable.

However, the best option is to combine the two if there is any question as to what you want your sum in life to be. Set a realistic "dead-line" and use the visualization of your memorial service to work backwards to fill in any blanks. Planning the service now offers a wealth of creative avenues for clarifying yourself to yourself. In *Thanatopics: Activities and Exercises for Confronting Death,* the authors suggest making a collage that gives priority to those aspirations or images you choose to represent your life, leaving space for those yet to come.

Another idea, "The Clothes We Wear," involves selecting your clothes for the service. This act may or may not help identify personal values and your chosen lifestyle. I really got into this exercise, torn between a white pantsuit and a high-necked, Victorian granny gown in turquoise or white. I was debating on footwear when I remembered I want to be cremated and have my ashes scattered in the Alps.

I favor "And the Music is You," a tape identifying those

musical selections that symbolize important experiences or periods in life. A few bars of some melodies can elicit deep feelings linked to an individual moment or relationship. Many have recurred, endured and bridged my life stages. Chronologically, the either constant or changing perspectives revealed in the lyrics are intriguing barometers of emotional maturing, ongoing or changing moods, and personalities. Buddha believed we are always changing and have no set identity, but I know *Mame* and Broadway showstoppers would be the alpha and omega refrain on my cassette. Those pews will rock as never before with Ethel Merman and Sammy Davis.

The Simontons report patients found especially helpful such imagery details as what they wished to express in closure to family and friends. I will have delivered a personal letter to each of the fifteen people close to me. I do not understand why more people do not write their own eulogies or create a personal statement or video. There is such therapy and relief in doing at least a statement *now* that reflects the aspirations, values, memories, those you love, whatever. It beats making sure your bed is made should an accident or stroke come tomorrow, and is, in fact, the best bedmaking you can leave behind.

The Simontons also reported that general patient reaction to the fantasy voyage through their own deaths was not at all as hard and distressing as they had expected! I can affirm this and reaffirm that the D-Day exercise is a motivating treasure.

Goodman's point is that premature death is not defined by chronology, that is, by how long a person has lived, but rather by how fully the individual has claimed the potentials of his or her *authentic* self. As such, "dying incomplete" attaches itself to long-lived fritterers who feel they wasted much or most of their lives through omission or commission. It may not apply necessarily to being snuffed out too soon—to living only a "season" due to terminal diseases or catastrophic events early in life. It does not apply to lack of time to achieve complete closure on good groundwork.

"Dying incomplete" applies more to not enough time left to right the ship, correct the course and, yes, to make amends. This is because if you are fulfilling your psychological needs, you can meet an early death and carry a feeling of completeness and self-esteem to it. But it is tough to breeze through the terminal stage at any age full of regrets and with lowered eyes. William James minced no words:

"To change one's life:
1) Start immediately.
2) Do it flamboyantly.
3) No exceptions."

Incompleteness due to early death

From this perspective, the premature death of a Mozart or Keats in their 30s was not as premature as it might have been for someone else of the same age. The young leukemia victim Ted Rosenthal wrote, "You can live a lifetime in a day; you can live a lifetime in a moment; you can live a lifetime in a year."[9] Dr. Elisabeth Kubler-Ross held that the meaning of a life can be fulfilled even if death comes in childhood.

In my reading I looked for academic, psychological and philosophical consensus and avoided specifically religious books, gurus and doctrines as sources. However, I admit my enthusiasm for the personal philosophy and psychology in a popular press book authored by a young, dying man. It won a 2002 Spiritual Book Award.

Philip Simmons was just 35 years old when he learned he had Lou Gehrig's disease and less than five years to live. A creative writing professor, writer, husband and father, Simmons offers remarkable insights in *Learning to Fall: The Lessons of an Imperfect Life*. On the road to inner peace, he found the first lesson is learning to let go. He points out that in the death and rebirth cycle throughout life, we must always first die to be reborn; and every death, every loss as he means it, requires a letting go—of preconceptions of unrealized potential and pride, of untied strings and plans, of ambition and ego, of relationships and health. "We let go of insisting that the world be a certain way. Letting go of any of these things can seem like the failure of every design, the loss of every cherished hope. But in letting go, we may also let go fear, let go our white-knuckled grip on a life that never seemed to meet our expectations, let go our anguished hold on our smaller selves our spirits have outgrown."

Buddhists have a firm hold on Letting Go of the Self and Its desires for Itself. The old adage is "You can't find the life that's waiting for you until you give up the one you have." As Simmons writes, you learn "when hitchhiking not to grasp your destination too firmly, lest you miss the journey." So it should be with preconceptions about roads and abilities left untried.

In the face of a shortened life, Simmons saw our goal as the ability, in the face of both tragedy and happiness, to return to the core of our highest selves. "We need to learn the art of returning home, returning to center, letting go of all that binds us too tightly to both fear and hope...letting go of our attachment to all that leaves us wobbling. When we learn to return home in this way, we will return bearing gifts."

Another major key Simmons held in releasing any regret and fear in the face of death is the realization that we are not separate from others. I suggest this frame of reference as the golden key to unlocking the toughest death anxiety early or late in life. Not only does this viewpoint undergird Eastern religions and cultures from India to Japan, it is the sermon preached by *all* world religions, namely that our identity and self-fulfillment is tied to that of our fellows here.

Simmons shares a feeling I myself have had, of being in a room, realizing everyone in it will die also and finding this feeling liberating. We are in this together, our true self-realization is stepping over the littleness of our "one" and into the ocean and fulfillment of all beings. He describes attending his children's piano recital and experiencing the sensation of playing the piano through them. No longer was there a distinction between "him" and "them"—they were playing the piano together: *For a few moments I broke through into what is called big mind, that state of being in which the illusion of our separateness falls away.*[10]

The phrase Big Mind resonates with me, unlike phrases such as the "collective unconscious," which conjures visions of a cold, primal soup. I will return to Big Mind's perspective in the belief that moving into it can be the most valuable death and rebirth knowledge in life. And, if we can practice the right deaths and rebirths during life, the final one will be a shoo-in.

Incompleteness in late life

An important point made by Dr. Gene Cohen in *The Creative Age* can be therapeutically applied to late-life despair at looking back and seeing a wasted field of years. His message is that there must be passage of time under our belts *first* if we are to have the experiences and opportunities needed for our human potential phases. "Midlife re-evaluation isn't something you can work ahead on at twenty-six."[11]

Fallow land is not barren, but inactive, ready and fertile and has been plowed in preparation for seed. Likewise, the long span of learning time behind us is an asset and framework for achievement of potentials and dreams. Cohen gives many examples of both famous and unknown late-in-life bloomers who creatively invented or reinvented themselves.

A particular hero of his is William Edmonson, an African American who lost his janitorial job in the 1930s during the Great Depression. He was inspired to take up carving as a coping mechanism. When he was 67 in 1937, he had the distinction of being the first Black artist in the history of New York's Museum of Modern Art to have a one-man show.

Another person Cohen mentions, a patient he saw for two years, is given as a prime example of the self-discovery and life reintegration possibilities of Dr. Butler's life review process. This patient, "Larry Carpenter," was 77 years old, retired from his own construction company, divorced for 33 years and uncomfortably distanced in his relationship with both grown children, particularly his son. Among his regrets were his work, which had never been all that fulfilling, and his inability to have nurturing relationships with women and his children.

Like his father, Carpenter had a habitual drinking problem to which he had returned upon the conviction that his life was a failure. His past revealed a stern parental upbringing and a series of teenage jobs from milk delivery and chauffeur to others such as bricklayer and roof repairer. These, along with engineering skills learned in the Army, prepared him well for ultimately starting his own construction company.

With the stress of remaining successful in his company and the demands of a family, he repeated the patterns of his father—emotional remoteness, severity, lofty expectations, excessive drinking. Divorce followed. Ongoing attempts of his children to better the situation when they had children resulted in drunken displays in front of his grandchildren, which only widened the chasm.

His life review brought Carpenter a new understanding and self-respect for his professional past. Cohen moved him beyond relapsing into his father's self-righteous attitudes and into the perspective of the loss to everyone if the situation were not ameliorated.

Cohen suggested a two-part plan: One, to write self-revealing, anecdotal letters to his grandchildren about each of his work experiences, such as "When Your Grandfather was a Teenage Shingle Layer." Through these written legacies, that would survive after his death, the grandchildren came to know him and their parents were reacquainted with their father. Second, Cohen suggested an alcohol rehabilitation program. Carpenter retrenched and regrouped along both lines and was able to reconnect, thereby hitting a homer in the ninth and gaining new self-respect.

As applied to feelings and fears of *incompleteness*, I quote, with emphasis, from Dr. Cohen's conclusion: "Larry had expressed with deep feeling that for the first time in his life he felt *whole*."[12] Part of Larry's feeling of completeness was the self-esteem and control gained in successfully confronting his addiction. The joy of self-esteem has everything to do with lessened death anxiety, and conquering an addiction is a sure-fire way to control it. One never learns how true this is, though, until the battle has been engaged.

We can take heart in James Ponet's example of Mr. Ten Commandments himself. "Moses standing atop Mount Nebo gazing wistfully across the Jordan into the land he will never enter—this is the signature of the Torah. *Not death itself, but incompletion haunts the man who has reached his life's limit.*"[13] Once in Deuteronomy 3:25, Moses beseeches God to let him cross over; but God answers, "I have let you see it with your own eyes, but you shall not cross there." (Deuteronomy 34:4)

We will never pack it all in.

---

[1] Taylor, Jeremy. *The Rule and Exercises of Holy Dying*. London: Richard Royston, 1651.

[2] American Heritage Dictionary, The.

[3] Goodman, Lisl Marburg, Dr. *Death and the Creative Life*. New York: Springer, 1981.

[4] Ibid., pp. 24-25.

[5] Armstrong, Karen. *The Spiral Staircase: My Climb out of Darkness*. New York & Toronto: Knopf, 2004, pp. xix-xx.

[6] Ibid. Presentation. "The Spiral Staircase." Westar Institute Spring Meeting. New York, 4-6 Mar. 2004.
[7] Shneidman, Edwin. *Voices of Death.* New York: Harper & Row, 1980, pp. 111-12.
[8] Butler, Robert N., M.D. "The Life Review: An Interpretation of Reminiscence in the Aged." *Psychiatry.* 26 (1963): 65-76. As cited in Gene D. Cohen, M.D., Ph.D. *The Creative Age: Awakening Human Potential in the Second Half of Life.* New York: Avon Books, 2000, pp. 241-42.
[9] Rosenthal, Ted. *How Could I Not Be Among You?* New York: George Braziller, 1973, p. 45.
[10] Simmons, Philip. *Learning to Fall: The Blessings of an Imperfect Life.* New York: Bantam, 2003. pp. 87, 141, 142, 76. (emphasis mine) NOTE: There is also a Big Mind process developed by Zen master Genpo Roshi.
[11] Cohen, Gene D., M.D., Ph.D. *The Creative Age: Awakening Human Potential in the Second Half of Life.* New York: Avon Books, 2000, pp. 1-16.
[12] Ibid., p. 245.
[13] Ponet, James E. "Reflections on Mortality from a Jewish Perspective." *Facing Death: Where Culture, Religion, and Medicine Meet.* Howard M. Spiro, Mary G. McCrea Curnen and Lee Palmer Wandel, eds. New Haven & London: Yale University Press, 1996, pp. 131-32. (emphasis mine)

Chapter 2

The Post-Self

> *To cease as though one has never been, to exit life with no hope of living on in the memory of another, to be obliterated, to be expunged from history's record—that is a fate literally far worse than death.*[1]

Goodman developed the concept of the fear of premature death, dying before we have actualized our potentials. For some death educators, Goodman's concept of the fear of dying incomplete or unrealized combines with the fears of separation and judgment in *the fear of extinction with insignificance.*

Humanity has, since before the days of the Pharaohs, sought to deny its mortality and transcend the fear of death by creating some way to continue. This innate drive to go on somehow is the antidote to the fear of the loss of self.

Some death educators hold it is not the loss of self man fears in our Western culture, but rather to die without having mattered.

The means humans have found to continue in some nonphysical way form *the concept of the post-self.*

It is taking the anxiety therapy which a purpose in life provides and saying that it is not enough. There remains also a narcissistic need "to leave some stain upon the silence," as Samuel Beckett put it. Death anxiety is assuaged not by what we think of ourselves but by what, if and how long others remember us.

More pronounced in Western societies which aggrandize the individual, it is a death-defying achievement succinctly explained in Samuel Butler's words, "He who is not forgotten is not dead."[2]

The current symbols of immortality which "give meaning to having lived" are

1. **Works**—the tangibles that continue to influence and impact lives—art, music, books; foundations, business, innovation, science.
2. **Genes**—generativity—biological immortality through children.
3. **Transplant into the body of others.**
4. **Memory held by others**—Shneidman[3] estimates this ability to have our actions count lasts about two generations.

The renowned Robert Jay Lifton, now of Harvard Medical School, also contributed that we can achieve a psychic connection with immortality in these additional modes:

5. **Theological**—the immortal soul; the ancient mythological symbol of death and rebirth. This rebirth into a death-transcending realm and truths, witnessed since primitive man, from the agricultural harvest to recent Native American mythology, is the thematic thread through Joseph Campbell's works.
6. **Natural**—Nature will remain, and a bit of ourselves remain with it. This is most often felt by those who exult in communion with nature, which gives them a sense of tranquillity, peace and spiritual fulfillment.
7. **The Special Mode of Experiential Transcendence**—as Lifton defined it, depends on a psychic state so intense that all awareness, senses and sense of mortality cease. *Losing oneself, one achieves ecstasy or rapture not just in mysticism*

> but in dance, song, athletic effort such as the runner's "zone," and artistic or intellectual creations. One feels different after this "high." This death-and-rebirth experience (while) *in life* is central to change and transformation. Lifton interpreted this state as one of extraordinary unity and perceptual intensity.[4]

It is among the first four choices that the individual's need to leave a self-preserving presence, some post-self trail of fame behind him, is seen in our society. However, my favorite story connected to these symbols involves the sixth one. Edwin Shneidman was in Japan where there is a deification of nature and an intimacy with it. He tells of addressing some Japanese students who asked for a reason why a person should not commit suicide if that person believed it resulted in becoming one with nature.[5]

In further opposition to American perspective and in stark contrast to American individualism is Lifton's study[6] of how the historically most prominent Japanese symbol of immortality is gained through personal meaning merging with the community's which will live on. *This involvement and identity with the ongoing community has lessened in modern times and* (individual) *death anxiety has increased.* He also notes the second mode of generativity, of immortality through children, is focal to China.

In 1988 the results of Mathews and Mister's questionnaire study,[7] an update related to Lifton's symbolic immortality work, were published. The study basically supported Lifton's modes as defined in five categories:

1. biological
2. theological
3. creative
4. natural
5. the special mode of experiential transcendence

However, there were several subtle and fascinating differences. Lifton saw the experiential mode as the choice of those who had lost faith in the future of mankind due to Hiroshima, genocide and so on. This emphasis was not substantiated by the study. Further, more respondents wanted generally pleasurable experiences rather than losing themselves in an intense experience.

Whereas Lifton had also included relationships (apart from genetic) in the biological mode, this study showed relationships to be considered in the creative mode, that is, a memory created which will live on in friends.

This study found that apparently the need for symbolic immortality is not as great as Lifton thought. It did substantiate, however, his sense of a growing psychic numbness, although not for the threatening nuclear reason he thought.

The study concluded that a clearer understanding of a person's needs for symbolic immortality (the need to be remembered) and how these needs can be met will, by consequence, make one's death easier to face.

According to the study, among the causes for our modern psychic numbness are the divorce rate, society impermanence and mobility of family ties, all of which lessen the chance of being remembered very long by kin.

The conclusion is that some crave and seek a post-self significance and some do not.

The Spanish philosopher and writer Miguel Unamuno was obsessed with post-self immortality, remarking, "Let me die, but let my fame live." He also gets my vote for best cut-to-the-chase theological assessment: "If there is no immortality, of what use is God?"

With an opposing opinion, we have the Nobel Prize-winning biologist James Watson: "I believe in Now. To hell with being discovered when you're dead." [8]

Getting Personal with Lifton's Modes

The artist-type...is driven by the fear of death to immortalize himself.
— **Otto Rank**, *Art and Artist*

WORKS: CREATIVE. Specifically, *creative differences* with respect to death anxiety. Goodman looks at creative people and finds that, although they too fear death, successful artists and scientists deal with these fears differently.

The greater the sense of achievement, the more prepared and positive they are towards death, *no matter what their chronological age.* (Among the population as a whole, death anxiety decreases in later mid-life.) Interestingly, given choices ranging from two to 1000 years after death, the highly creative group interviewed had little or no desire to return nor any interest in visiting any previous period. Future-oriented, they didn't dwell on the past. They were less afraid of death than the general population.

One difference appears to be that artists, such as musicians, think less about death; scientists, more. But both are generally at peace. Although a rudimentary study and not conclusive, these findings do indicate a direct correlation between creative accomplishment and lowered death anxiety.

If Goodman's thesis is accepted, how could this be surprising? What false note could come between the soul of the artist and his brush's stroke on the canvas? The creative person connects intimately with authentic potentials and when these are successfully realized in work, life can be considered "complete." Both an authentic life and post-self immortality have been attained.

Leo Tolstoy exemplified the angst driving the artist type to a post-self existence, and his characters are, in my opinion, literature's most profoundly drawn examples of death confrontations. "What will become of my whole life?" Tolstoy writes. "Is there any meaning in my life that the inevitable death awaiting me does not destroy?"[9] Appropriate reflections of their author's drive to immortalize himself, Tolstoy's works were vast archetypal landscapes whose iconic themes escaped the dimensions of time and setting.

What, though, of the *un*successful artist-type? Oliver Hailey's contemporary play *For the Use of the Hall* sends a message to those whose creative works are their vocation and who suffer the curse of evaluated creative failures. The play concerns just such types, and one in particular, a playwright. After the opening of his latest and greatest ignominious flop, he is exalted by a dream of a gentle *Times* review. In it the critic claimed a sympathetic kinship with the playwright and told him he should feel only pleasure and gratitude "for the use of the Hall." After his and other characters' deaths, the play concludes that there are no wasted lives—Enjoy!

I recall seeing this play and wishing that seeing were believing. The greatest highs and lowest lows are known by the creative person who works in solitude and who will identify closely with the reception the work will receive. As Alan Jay Lerner put it, "I have come to realize that I write not because it is what I do, but because it is what I am; not because it is how I make my living, but it is how I make my life."[10] Indeed, generally the creative type has his purpose in life tightly tied up with his work. His "drive to immortalize himself" is out there on a high wire without the safety net of family and other ego-boosting options others perceive necessary to be on a more equal basis.

Another perspective for those with a résumé of artistic or any other professional failures is far more serious therapy than the message of Hailey's play. It is Joseph Addison's claim, " 'Tis not in mortals to command success, / But we'll do more, Sempronius,—we'll deserve it."[11] Surely that is a far more just yardstick by which to judge success and failure, since so often the difference between the two in reality is merely the luck of circumstances. Addison's line has my vote to go to the top of a list of death-education axioms. We can never control a success that has the component of outside affirmation, but we can control whether or not we deserve it. Understanding that goes a long way towards inner peace.

WORKS: BUSINESS. Defined as business endeavors, foundations and so on.

Schemer and promoter P. T. Barnum was perishing to know what people would say about him after he died. Word got around, and the *New York Evening Sun* accommodated him by publishing on May 24, 1891, a four-column obituary headlined, "Great and Only Barnum. He wanted to read his Obituary; Here It Is."[12]

Privileged and brilliant Swedish industrialist Alfred Nobel also looked down the road toward his obituary. As the story goes, he was upset at a prospective post-self image focused on his invention of dynamite. He was devoted to peace efforts, wrote poetry and dramas, and had even thought of a career change—to writer. Thus it was that a year before he died of a cerebral hemorrhage in 1896, he changed his will. His fortune endowed the Nobel Institute prizes in Peace, Literature, Medicine, Physics, Chemistry and Economics.

At least one of these men handled his foreseen post-self fame and place in history well.

A suggestion: A doable amount left in one's will not generically for a favored cause, but for a small component, a specific unmet need we have uncovered or conceived, can be one of the most therapeutic and *creative* gifts to ourselves.

Another tangible legacy is a document called an *ethical will*. It contains the values and life lessons a person wants to bequeath and is a terrific, significant means of living on.

GENES. In the years I have researched and pondered these subjects, I have concluded that this mode of immortality provides huge satisfaction and softens death anxiety for a great many in our culture with close ties to their children. Regarding the importance of this Biological mode and that of Memory as endorsed by others, the specific emotion of love may be the most indelible, enduring and frequently recalled.

THE SPECIAL MODE OF EXPERIENTIAL TRANSCENDENCE. Some of the best examples of transforming death-and-rebirth experiences appear in American mythic tales of the great cinematic *auteurs*. Often, this is the core of a script's character development. Noteworthy are the films of Frank Capra.

In what could be called a Jesus myth, *Mr. Smith Goes to Washington*, reference is made to "crucifying" James Stewart's Jefferson Smith. The parallel of suffering, crucifixion and revival-resurrection in life culminates during the final scene in the Senate. Moreover, the opposing Judas-Pontius Pilate character is a superb example of a spiritual death-and-rebirth spiritual transformation. Pointed reference is also made to the angry crowd "crucifying" John Doe in *Meet John Doe*. Then there are the climactic crucifixion parallels in *Mr. Deeds Goes to Town* (complete with your basic "Sermon on the Mount") and in *It's a Wonderful Life*. In *Lost Horizon*, the transformative experience in the snowstorm of Ronald Coleman's character is a metaphoric death-and-rebirth return to Shangri-la. Equally a classic tale of the hero's Individuation journey, it commences with Separation from the Known, through trials and revelations, to a transformation of consciousness that ensures the hero's return.

Capra's innocent, idealistic heroes stood for American patriotism and waved it inspiringly in the face of Fascism's threat in World War II. His films embody many of the themes in this section. For example, two modes—"Memory held by others" and "Works"—are precisely what *It's a Wonderful Life* is all about! The mark George Bailey learns that his life has made on everyone in an entire town touched and continues to pluck a resonant American chord in a manner unparalleled for over fifty years. *It's a Wonderful Life* powerfully spread out for the audience to absorb the issue that an ordinary man mattered. Most of Capra's heroes come out of the chute fully evolved into authentic selfhood. All were motivated and acted from their "authentic" centers with the hope of moving the audience likewise.

No theme was more dramatically realized than the death-and-rebirth climaxes. In real life, there can be multiple death and rebirths. Examples can range from symbolic rites of passage, to loss and regeneration milestones, to consciousness altering and spiritually enlightening moments or events, quietly experienced, alone. A mother might name the experience of her baby's birth and bonding. That ranks highest in my life.

THEOLOGICAL AND NATURAL. In what activity as a child did Joseph Campbell lose all sense of time? Following his fascination with Native American folklore and culture! That bliss-filled preoccupation as a child indeed forecast the mythic journey of his life.

In *The Mirror of Time*, Boyle and Morriss describe the Hopi Indian concept of death as an ongoing cycle and balance between the two worlds. Their legends reflect the return down through the *sipapu*, a giant hollow reed in the earth, a symbolic womb of rebirth, to the lower world of their origin where they belong. This continuity through death and return is exemplified also by their *tense-less language:* both the future and the past are ever-present. Past events are judged by their emotional intensity, not chronological place in history.[13]

Native Americans connect deism to nature's rhythms and forces. In New Mexico the Pueblo Indians originally dug pit houses for protection, from which they would emerge with the rising sun, a veritable rebirth daily out of the womb.

Like the Pueblo people, I find in the ground and sky all

my sacred symbols. I find my closest communion with immortal possibilities, not in the volcanic mountains to which these Native Americans go for instruction, but at chosen spots in the Alps where I experience a deep sense of belonging. It was, however, in the western United States while I sat one day in a vast preserve, contemplating a screen of green mountains, that these words came to me, "As long as this exists, there is no death." It is a mantra I repeat now whenever a spot finds me that I want to imprint in memory.

This is not pantheism, for I do not equate deism and nature. Rather nature for me is the Connector to Something Else, to the mystery which all of man's attempts have failed to collar and define adequately. Campbell once defined a myth as a bridge between the visible and the invisible planes. For me, nature is that bridge and holds affirming intimations of immortality. Two such natural symbols are metaphors of continuity.

I came upon a redwood tree over 1500 years old, all burned out inside. Yet it still survived. A companion whose husband had just endured massive chemotherapy treatments made a profound connection with that tree. The buried roots had outlived fire to inspire new growth. The seeds of nature's tallest child fall off like acorns, but those rarely germinate. Rather, new trees begin with sprouts of the broad roots, just about ten feet below the surface. Those roots need the community of redwoods around them to survive. Interdependent, like the human community.

Ecosystems are only healthy if they have many diverse species, like the human community. After wind and fire, the forest gives way, and in a blink healthier versions and fresh flowering species move into the space. Indeed, the seeds of one pine rest imprisoned in the tree's resin-encased cones. Like Sleeping Beauty, they may wait for lifetimes until the melting heat of a fire releases them to spread as saplings in the newly enriched soil.

On a beach walk I see the same regenerative cycle in the ebb and tide of the ocean's waves. A wave resembles a human life. I watch the white crescendo as it rolls to my feet, then dominoes down the beach. I am mesmerized as each wave is sucked back and under to support and join the next coming along after.

Only part of the tree gives way; the roots survive and sprout beneath. Only part of the wave is spent; some measure of it returns with the next wave. Death is physical and visible and is in the eye of the beholder. It is what one cannot see just beneath the surface that reinvents itself and returns again. The "What if…"

Jung wrote of a plant as symbol in his memoirs. "I have never lost a sense of something that lives and endures underneath the eternal flux. What we see is the blossom, which passes. The rhizome remains."[14]

Nature is my favorite symbolic mode of immortality.

Gertrude

As a concluding comment on the post-self, I offer the following case study of one who felt the need to be a "Person," to stand out and be noted for singular high accomplishment, who needed to be indispensable.

Hers was not a kindly nature. Indeed, her biographer Janet Wallach says some called Gertrude Bell arrogant, imperious and ambitious. Born in 1868, she was the first woman to graduate from Oxford with a First in Modern History. She possessed the snobbism of money, the support and haughtiness of a doting aristocratic family, the assertive intimidation of her intellectual brilliance. Bell authored a prolific number of acclaimed books, articles and a white paper on the Middle East. She dismissed most women as inferiors.

She was the only female appointed Political Officer in

World War I and afterwards Oriental Secretary. Also, she received the Royal Geographic Society's Gold Medal and Commander of the Order of the British Empire.

She learned Arabic and the surveying skills of a cartographer, as well as camel riding and tent etiquette so she might dine correctly with sheiks in remote desert interiors. She was a gifted archeologist whose collection formed the base of the world-renowned Baghdad Museum which, as fledgling Iraq's Director of Antiquities, she founded. In great part due to Bell's substantive information and intimate friendships with them, both T. E. Lawrence and King Faisal assumed their places in power and history.

A prolific letter writer, especially to her father whom she worshipped, Bell helped her eventual biographer enormously to uncover the inner torment as the survivor of several heartbreaking relationships. An atheist, when young she had belittled her brother when he took the Church as vocation. However, on his death she wrote, "The thing which comes uppermost is that he had a *complete* life. His perfect marriage and the joy of his children."[15]

In her own eyes, Gertrude Bell was never *complete*. Even as the loving marriage and children she yearned for eluded her, she defensively fought to be a Person of Consequence instead, both in a world of men and as an indispensable force in Iraq's creation. Finally, the time came when her role was expendable. In 1926, at the age of 57, Gertrude Bell took an overdose of sleeping pills rather than return, as she perceived, incomplete and only half a Person, to Britain and her beloved family. Although her family's fortune had severely dwindled, she left 50,000 pounds to the Baghdad Museum. The Museum today houses a major wing bearing her name, and there, in the basement, "on a forgotten shelf, a bronze bust of Miss Gertrude Bell waits to be dusted off."[16]

This is the biographical portrait which Wallach paints in

Desert Queen. The publisher asserts on the back cover that, at the time of her death, she was "the most powerful woman in the British Empire." Without editorial comment, I propose Gertrude Bell as a Case for Thought to conclude this discussion of the Post-Self.

---

[1] Shneidman, Edwin. *Deaths of Man*. New York: Quadrangle/The New York Times Book Co., 1973, p. 52.

[2] Rowe, Dorothy. *The Construction of Life and Death*. Chicester: John Wiley, 1982, Beckett & Butler quotes, p. 37.

[3] Shneidman. Op. cit., p. 43.

[4] Lifton, Robert Jay. *The Broken Connection: On Death and the Continuity of Life*. New York: Simon & Schuster, 1979.

[5] Shneidman. Op. cit., p. 68.

[6] Lifton, Robert Jay, et al. *Six Lives, Six Deaths: Portraits from Modern Japan*. New Haven & London: Yale University Press, 1979.

[7] Mathews, Robert C., and Rena D. Mister. "Measuring an Individual's Investment in the Future: Symbolic Immortality, Sensation Seeking, and Psychic Numbness." *Omega: Journal of Death and Dying*. Robert J. Kastenbaum, Ph.D., ed. Farmingdale, NY; Baywood. 18.3 (1987-88): 161-73.

[8] Shneidman. Op. cit., pp. 45-46.

[9] Tolstoy, Leo. *Confessions*. (1882). London: Oxford, 1961, p. 24.

[10] Lerner, Alan Jay. *The Street Where I Live*. (1978). Cambridge & New York: Da Capo Press, 1994.

[11] Addison, Joseph. *Cato: A Tragedy in Five Acts*. 1713. I. ii. 43.

[12] Forbes, Malcolm, with Jeff Block. *They Went That-a-Way*. New York: Simon & Schuster, 1988.

[13] Boyle, Joan M., and James E. Morriss. *The Mirror of Time: Images of Aging and Dying*. New York: Greenwood, 1987, pp. 7-9.

[14] Wehr, Gerhard. *Jung: A Biography*. Boston: Shambhala, 1987, p. 454.

[15] Wallach, Janet. *Desert Queen: The Extraordinary Life of Gertrude Bell—Adventurer, Adviser to Kings, Ally of Lawrence of Arabia*. (1996) New York: Anchor Books Edition, 1999, p. 368. (emphasis mine)

[16] Ibid., p. 377.

Chapter 3

The Real Self

> *So many lives, lived as a result of fixed decisions, victims of the inequalities and failures of education, employment, economic support, and marriage, are wasteful in comparison to what they might have been....In my experience as a clinician, I find that people seem to regret most what they did not do rather than what they did.*[1]

I, for one, can look back on many floundering years. When a friend once cheeringly assured me that Capricorns are late bloomers, I reminded her I am a Virgo.

Late- and Never-Bloomers

This chapter and the following one address this prevalent life situation which Dr. Robert Butler, first Director of the National Institute on Aging and pioneer of life review therapy, describes in his Pulitzer Prize-winning book *Why Survive?* He laments the forced identities, secret lives, and those who live pseudo lives who withdraw from danger.

Among these acting and role playing their empty lives away are homosexuals in denial and those who do not believe in what they are doing for reasons of income or social standing. There are also those with "lives of quiet desperation." All of these comprise the late-bloomers and never-bloomers for whom death anxiety may be particularly intense. Here are characteristics which many of those of this description lack.

A diffused sense of identity plays out as inability to take mature courses of action and commitment regarding career, life steps or relationships. James Masterson defines capacities of the real self thus: "to spontaneously activate the self with supportive self-assertion, to acknowledge self-worth and self-activation and mastery, to feel self-entitlement, to be able to soothe intense affects, to identify the self's unique individuated wishes and activate them in reality, to make and pursue a commitment, and to be creative."[2] Commitment and the spontaneous act are vital signs of the real self. Once again, these themes fill the mythic tales of all the great cinematic *auteurs*. Here is Sander Lee's comparison between principals in the films of Alfred Hitchcock and Woody Allen.

"In *Rear Window*, as in many other Hitchcock films, existential themes are clearly articulated. In both *Rear Window* and [Allen's] *Manhattan Murder Mystery*, the protagonist is initially portrayed in bad faith, afraid to become committed to anything. In the course of each film, that person is faced with a series of challenges, often life-threatening, which act as a catalyst in bringing that person into authentic being. The realization of the possibility of death (nonbeing) calls the conscience of the individual to an acceptance of authenticity. The protagonist is faced with a situation in which a fundamental choice must be made. In making that choice, the protagonist becomes engaged in life and, at least temporarily, overcomes bad faith. Hitchcock equates the achievement of authentic selfhood with the ability to successfully establish a romantic link with another person."[3]

Lee chose a good example in *Rear Window*'s L. B. Jeffries. A photographer, he has eluded commitments in his own life by viewing and photographing others. By becoming responsibly and emotionally involved in events outside his rear window, he overcomes his escapism. In contrast, Lee notes that

Allen's characters in *Manhattan Murder Mystery* as well as in *Husbands and Wives* do not go through the same catharsis or emerge with the possibility of authentic romantic commitment.

Goodman has found that whether or not a person thinks often or little of one's death is not a determining factor. She voices the consensus that seeing and claiming death on a personal level rather than as an external force is instead a determinant of lessened death anxiety as well as a mark of authenticity. Only after we are in touch with our authentic nature are we able to integrate its ultimate loss in a therapeutic, anxiety-relieving way.

As an adult you must rediscover the moving power of your life. "Tension, a lack of honesty and a sense of unreality come from following the wrong force in life," stated Joseph Campbell.[4] The outcome of following the wrong force can include following a false self, which is the disturbing reality for a significant number of us who are out of touch with our feelings. No purpose in life will be meaningful and assuage death anxiety unless the true self, acting upon authentic feelings, is functioning.

Ironically, the real self is a phenomenon of change. It is healthy to have different sides bundled in the same personality and to have an identity which evolves and does not stay locked into old, stale choices. Feelings mature, tastes change and psychological needs are always responding to new directions and stimuli. The real self can fluidly follow these without breaking up base camp!

In support of this view, Butler does not agree completely with Erik Erikson's affirmation of consolidating one's identity for the long haul. Although he does not favor complete diffusion of personality, he is skeptical of a preoccupation with efforts to maintain identity, which really "amounts to a rather systematic renunciation of ourselves and our possibilities."[5]

The second half of the 20th century saw stunning

advances in death education and behavioral psychology. Regarding the latter, mental and emotional stability was once measured by maintaining commitments and consistent identity roles. Here, though, are Butler's words, written back in 1975, including a popular phrase he may have coined.

Human beings need the freedom to live with change, to invent and reinvent themselves a number of times throughout their lives. By loosening up life we enlarge the value of the gift of life.[6]

Extra Steps for Two Profiles

The next chapter addresses specific individuation components: ego, circumstance, luck and finding a meaningful purpose that affects the real self's coping ability with death anxiety.

First, in this chapter, are two profiles of impaired bloomers for which rudimentary therapy is needed before these next issues can be properly integrated. One is a common childhood tragedy which can impinge on the ability to

1. activate potentials that have one's own handwriting on them
2. find meaningful use of life time
3. confront the fears of death successfully

James McCarthy connects the fear of death to a higher incidence among women and the degree of anxiety to separation conflicts, i.e., "wishes for separation—individuation, fears of abandonment, and corollary wishes or fears of psychic merger and fusion." He sees the terror of abandonment's first manifestations "in the infant and young child's experience with the mother....The relationship with the mother either restrains death anxiety or allows it to grow."[7]

Locating the authentic person inside requires confronting and separating from any persona created by the childhood demands of parents, ideally in a communicative therapeutic setting. "The Search for the True Self" is the subtitle Alice Miller gave *The Drama of the Gifted Child*. This famed, remarkable book focuses on the child whose spontaneous, authentic needs and characteristics are never mirrored by the parent. Rather *the child is the mother's possession, and its needs are replaced with the parent's own needs. The child is rewarded with love and acceptance to the degree it fulfills the parent's model.* The result is an adult alienated from self, often exhibiting forms of narcissistic disturbances, namely grandiosity and depression, and "grandiosity is the defense against depression, and depression is the defense against the deep pain over the loss of the self that results from denial." [8] The denial is of the authentic nature that was never mirrored in childhood, that was suppressed.

Miller further states, "*One is free from [depression] only when self-esteem is based on the authenticity of one's own feelings and not the possession of certain qualities.*" The house comes falling down when there is a threat and collapse of self-esteem, which, in the grandiose person, is quite precarious since his or her self-respect is dependent on the admiration of others and qualities (such as beauty) and accomplishments, any or all of which can fail at any time. Of course, depression can often follow. *Aging, and the fears of losing one's looks and increasing disfigurement in the dying stage can be just such triggers.*

Indeed, Michael Kearl in his in-depth sociological study of death and dying *gives the fear of physical disfigurement* (the loss of a lot of weight, hair and the like in a terminal illness or its treatment) as *a primary fear of dying alongside the fears of dependency, loneliness, pain, and loss of dignity.* [9]

Specifically, Miller gives the instance of an unmarried woman who needed constant affirmation of her good looks which had served her as a substitute for the mirroring she had missed from her mother. Superficially, her depression might appear the result of lack of sexual contacts, but "at a deeper level *early fears of being abandoned were now aroused*, and this woman had no new conquests with which to counteract them."[10] The lack of mirroring in childhood and the resulting lack of an authentic self can be, on its own, the cause of heightened death anxiety.

I recall growing up with no idea, even in college and for long afterwards, what my identity was to myself or to others. I was desperate to find or create one! The light never went on to feel through what and who made me happy, angry, affirmed, defensive, fulfilled creatively, ashamed and so on. Daydreams filled my teenage loneliness and would return occasionally whenever I was alone for many years. Finally, I distanced myself, geographically, over a thousand miles from my family. The daydreams disappeared and my depression with them. For the first time in over a decade, I was able to cry. It was wonderful.

In sum, as a dutiful mama's girl, I had failed either to separate or to be the desired clone. When a therapist explained my parents had rejected me (something they would never understand), it took years to comprehend. The therapy was to get in touch with my feelings and to do grief work. I practiced replacing "I think" in my sentences with "I feel." I went down a painful but necessary memory road.

I always had an increasing dread of growing old and losing my looks, which reflected the lack of mirroring and the fear of abandonment. Now my wrinkles carelessly abound. When I had some small implants and, for the second time, high-risk breast tissue removed, it never occurred to me to want to reconstruct. I will admit I have not seen my natural hair color in decades. Question: If my natural color is brunette and my feelings go for silver, which is the authentic self? Silver—an easy bliss call.

The same person described here and in the Preface also heard herself called a narcissist under someone's breath!

Although that someone did not know me at all, she had nailed my fragile surface veneer perfectly. For at the same time I was escaping into daydreams, my creative, grandiose side was occasionally and without sustainable direction, winning honors for a play, a television concept, leadership programs for disadvantaged youth and on and on. I felt bored, empty and weary beyond my years.

Believing I was superior and meant for great things, I was on permanent hold as to the where, what and how. I was needy for that missing, affirming, maternal mirroring. I sought it to some extent from my husband and then later, from my children, particularly my daughter.

I was privileged throughout those years to have about a dozen truly extraordinary women friends who remain among my closest friends today. When things fell apart, when the anger and despair started tumbling out, they never walked away.

Why bother with my story? Because I am a textbook case. Legions of us lacked mirroring for any number of parental circumstances and fear abandonment. We still may be estranged from our true selves and suffering heightened fears of death. I suspect a strong number of us would agree with the general statement that our parent or parents were good, well-intentioned people, who—like many of us in our turn next as parents—fell short "in some way."

Another profile study for death anxiety is one I researched separately. I wanted to learn if there might be spiritual demons unique to terminally ill, long-term, substance abusers. Nothing can take a person farther away from what he or she could have been than an addiction. I wanted to know if therapeutic intervention might yet be possible for their sense of wasted lives.

Specifically, my choice for focus was the early onset alcoholic. Age at death aside, alcohol is cited as the third-most-frequent cause of death in the United States, which should give the subject of its spiritual devastation an inextricable place in death education and counseling. Regarding geriatric alcoholics, reportedly over four million elderly Americans abuse alcohol. This number can be viewed as arbitrary when you consider that an estimated 80-90% of our elderly problem drinkers go undetected! For reasons, add the factors of retirement and living alone to doctors' misreading of alcohol abuse for those of ordinary aging. A number of elderly, terminally ill alcoholics have advanced dementia and, disengaged, are beyond reach regardless of whether or not their terminal illness was a direct result of alcohol abuse.

In death education, emphasis is placed on the relationship between a) social interaction and b) the general physical and emotional well-being of both those with failing health and the bereaved. The principle of this equation holds in studies of geriatric alcoholism. In fact, statistics show that elderly abusers who join support groups such as Senior AA, have a *notably* lower rate of recidivism than their younger counterparts.

Surprisingly, once past the high hurdle of initial commitment, there is some evidence, though inconclusive, that late versus early onset is not a determining point! The so-little-time-left factor and the desire for close social connectedness in the ongoing peer group are, rather, compelling propellants to sustained recovery. In spite of regrets about wasted years and an impaired self unable to realize potentials, the substance abuser who claims victory each day over addiction is rightly flooded with self-esteem which, as in Larry Carpenter's case, brings a sense of completeness, even at a late age.

But what of the spiritual plight of one for whom time has shut the door for such rehabilitation? I spoke with Dr. Ernest Noble, Director of UCLA's Alcohol Research Center who has been at the forefront of genetic studies related to alcoholism as well as to other substance abuse. He explained that findings strongly point to two types of alcoholics.

The Real Self

The milder case develops over time from chronic, excessive drinking. The more toxic form has a genetic base. Simplified, evidence shows the presence of the A1 allele of the dopamine receptor gene in a disproportionately high number of severely alcoholic cases, with logic indicating the remainder attributable to environmental and/or other gene factors. Sober, these genetically predisposed majority of alcoholics *feel crummy and out of kilter*. Vulnerable to their first drink, this is the type more likely to be in lifelong denial or repeated losers in rehabilitation attempts.

The A1 allele in the DRD2 gene has been linked as well to cocaine, obesity and smoking. Environmental factors and gender also appear to play a determining role. It is surmised the A1 allele may cause a deficiency in the dopaminergic system. An individual who uses alcohol, nicotine, cocaine and food to compensate releases dopamine which activates these areas.

Imbalances in a person's biochemistry are corrected for such disorders as bipolarism, largely with great success. A medical problem requires in addition to a medical solution the removal of social stigmata and consequent family denial.

Several drugs hold promise for substance addictions. If a molecular basis is substantiated for certain substance addictions *and accepted sympathetically by the general public*, will it change how the non-recovered addict feels about himself or herself in the face of dying? Will those of us in their families *whose own potentials have been impaired* be able to give up deeply embedded anger and recriminations and reach out to their anxiety with the words, "It has not been your fault"? For decades medical science has pointed to alcoholism and other addictions as a medical problem, not a moral one. But for those practicing addicts and their families, this may not be therapy enough when facing the loss of potentials that never were realized.

It is a situation I know well. To this day no one has

topped my father's straight-*A* academic record at a leading university as well as his being first to graduate with a Master's of Law. President of his fraternity, distinguished war veteran, Vice President of a major international oil company, Sunday School teacher and supervisor. Handsome. How much I would have loved to know the real him. Early onset alcoholism.

Ultimately, his professional colleagues checked him into a hospital. I understand his blood alcohol level on entry showed him to be as close to an alcoholic coma as any addict this huge detox unit had ever admitted while the patient was still conscious. Admission was at 8 A.M. He was 76. That he never took another drink for his remaining eight years is a moot point. His mind had fuzzed permanently. There was no closure to unfinished business, and open wounds were left behind.

Before they can confront their fears of death successfully, those with forced, pseudo and impaired identities *first* need to take an extra step and return home to their real selves.

---

[1] Butler, Robert N., M.D. *Why Survive? Being Old in America.* New York: Harper & Row, 1975, pp. 398-99.
[2] Masterson, James F., M.D. *The Real Self: A Developmental, Self, and Object Relations Approach.* New York: Brunner-Mazel, 1985, p. 31.
[3] Lee, Sander H. *Woody Allen's Angst: Philosophical Commentaries on His Serious Films.* Jefferson, NC, & London: McFarland, 1997, p. 345.
[4] Osbon, Diane K., ed. *A Joseph Campbell Companion: Reflections on the Art of Living.* New York: Harper-Collins, 1991, p. 182.
[5] Butler. Op. cit., p. 400.
[6] Ibid. Op. cit., p. 401.
[7] McCarthy, James B. *Death Anxiety: The Loss of the Self.* New York: Gardner, 1980, pp. 189-90.
[8] Miller, Alice. *The Drama of the Gifted Child: The Search for the True Self.* Rev. Ed. New York: Basic Books, 1994, p. 58.
[9] Kearl, Michael C. *Endings: A Sociology of Death and Dying.* New York & Oxford: Oxford University Press, 1989, pp. 487-88.
[10] Miller. Op. cit., pp. 58-61. (emphasis mine)

CHAPTER 4

PRESCRIPTIONS

Rarely is life a gathering success story.

As Laura Hillenbrand writes in *Seabiscuit*, the horse's trainer, Tom Smith, was a penniless horseman who at 56 "appeared to have reached the end of the road"[1] and never had a good break on it—until he was given a chance to train a racehorse few had any hope for. Red Pollard, the horse's rider, had been abandoned as a young boy, then never succeeded as a prizefighter or as a jockey. He, too, found a mentor in the horse's owner.

Their spans of success and recognition were not long, less than five years in Pollard's case. Pollard ended up polishing boots at the racetrack, enduring more injuries and dying in a nursing home. After Seabiscuit's retirement, Smith went on to be a great trainer for Elizabeth Arden Graham until an unverified incident unfairly tarnished his reputation. He died in a sanitorium with few but his family to mourn him. Both men had slipped back into obscurity.

As for the horse, Seabiscuit didn't win until his 17th race, and it wasn't until his 50th start that he really caught on to racing. He might never have had the chance to give the best that was in him had he not had a trainer who knew to listen to him, his rhythms and unique responses and patiently support the horse in finding his own way. It is easy to anthropomorphize Seabiscuit and his path of development, as well as the racecourse and its rich language as symbols of a life's course—from a bad start out of the gate to breaking down in the home stretch.

I am grateful Hillenbrand revived this Depression-Era story to bestseller status. Not only are these three mythic figures—Pollard, Smith, and the Biscuit—applicable to the issue of realizing potentials but also to luck, which includes circumstances such as adequate peer reinforcement and, professionally, a mentor's hand up. The words of Red Pollard's daughter, Norah Christianson, spell it out perfectly.

My father understood that it was just by chance that he became famous. So many millions have talent or beauty and they haven't been in the right place at the right time and they haven't drifted into an arena where they'd be appreciated. I think he knew that very deeply that it was all luck.[2]

Luck, the critical determinant, does not exist according to one philosophy. Through certain choices, we create and follow patterns that either enhance or defeat the self. I do not agree, and I am a walking wealth of examples.

I created a boxed stationery item of humorous notecards. Neiman-Marcus bought a certain quantity for an exclusive introduction in a Christmas catalogue, and I promised an ample, ready, backup number. My award-winning designer had never created stationery. He came up with a custom envelope size which I, as an amateur, did not question. The cost of the custom die was exorbitant and wiped out a profit margin. For the first time ever, something went wrong with that catalogue's run. It went out to only a fraction of its regular circulation, the marketplace equivalent of an act of God. Produced as a catalogue item, the notecards had no second life in a store since the contents of the sealed box were hidden. *Luck? No, an expensive, deflating, learning experience.*

On a commission corporate job, I first sat down with the department administrator, and we agreed on and drew up a budget. Months later, after I had worked my ass off to bring in an unexpectedly large amount, I discovered in the file that the budget had since been redone, halving my commission. The administrator explained, "I didn't know you needed the money. You once had on an ultra-suede dress." I had not insisted on a signed contract against that first budget. The paper copy I had of it and my childish trust were meaningless. *Luck? No! It was the old setting-yourself-up-to-be-a-victim pattern.*

I co-owned a children's bookmark company with the head of an advertising agency. The agency-created bookmarks were innovative and adorable. I did a great job of setting up national bookstore and gift store representatives, who quickly reported back that few stores wanted the bookmarks because they were not durable enough. Bad choice of partner? No, the agency was award-winning and had made weight and laminating decisions on paper materials for sturdy, permanent displays. Was I repeating a deep-seated pattern and setting myself up to be a victim? No. *My Luck.*

Reliving these memories would be indulgent if they were not tied to heightened death anxiety. Bad luck and self-defeating patterns can affect self-esteem, thereby acting as a growth hormone for the "worm." Certainly I can relate to the two in my case.

Proposed Prescription: A national recovery group for Badly Lucked And Patterned people. BLAP! Seriously? At least half-seriously! These are hard experiences to take out of the closet. The therapy of releasing them to others and, in cases of victim-creating patterns, working through them with their support can bring a transforming catharsis.

Surely humor and group morale will keep up attendance. Instead of a prayer, the BLAP meetings could start with a rousing rendition of "Luck Be a Lady Tonight." Instead of a chip, as is given at an AA meeting to honor length of time of sobriety, a pair of BLAP dice could be given to commemorate testimony of changing luck or a winning situation. I can see the slogan now: *Kick the Patterns with BLAP Anonymous.*

More seriously, this chapter is all about when favorable circumstances and luck are missing. It is about detours and finding meaning anyway. Here are two propositions that underpin the text.

ONE. Even if Joseph Campbell rightly moans in his grave, consider the possibility of the flexibility of bliss and *the bliss of the moment.* We are always changing. To focus on what this moment holds is the Buddhist way. What, in each moment, makes the best of it alone? Recognizing and experiencing the bliss of the moment is an alternate concept of bliss to follow. Few see the possibilities the present moment offers them.

The flexibility of bliss can also refer to the longer term, wide-angled bliss which is both a means of traveling and a direction. It presumes that there may be an optimal path on which all of one's unique cylinders fire. It also presumes that there is more than one avenue for filling *enough* of an individual's psychological needs to give that life both purpose and esteem and thus defend against the fear of dying.

Intellectually, I know my path, according to Campbell's lexicon, lies in creative expression. Emotionally, though, my young son wanting to play Monopoly® with me, and then, as a grown man, wanting to be off work and with me when I was visiting brought even deeper feelings of bliss than any acceptance of a creative project ever has or could.

With a change of perspective, a person's unique potentials for completion can come together behind a different storefront than one that was idealized. Feelings, like instincts, come from the same spontaneous source, the real self. In that instant, both are filtered through what we call conscience, which issues a "prick" in the form of shame, usually if the feeling is not ennobling.

Point: Finding "bliss" through *feelings* and making a commitment to the positive ones opens a much broader space with more creative wiggle room for expression than *thinking* where "bliss" defines itself, which is often a narrow space without windows or doors to other possibilities.

In sum, *being in touch with one's entire range of positive feelings, spontaneity and creativity is the real self, blooming and strutting its full scope of potentials.* A kaleidoscope of reconfigurations becomes open to it. Picturing the kaleidoscope as metaphor, its reconfigurations carry all the same, beautiful elements. The components are simply re-arranged to express themselves in a different formation in order to accommodate the reality of circumstances. As will be seen in the insights regarding coping with an actual terminal diagnosis, seeing options, perspective and the power of choice are everything.

TWO. Consider Goodman's deduction, based on her many interviews with artists, scientists and "ordinary" people. She observed that people whose work is an end in itself have less fear of dying than do those who view their work as a means to an unrelated end, as 9-to-5 work as a financial means elsewhere would be, for example. This is a tremendous *Alert,* not necessarily to leave an assembly line with great family health benefits, but rather an Alert to motivate a new evaluation of time invested around the job and possibilities within the job itself.

Any job involving other people has creative potential for the best in us. And anything that activates the best in us, activates meaning and esteem. Meaning and esteem are the "end" goal, not the means to it! Being "in the moment," mindful of that altered perspective, is important.

Some notions bred by Western individualism feed death anxiety and are fit for the trash can. For example, the notion still exists that a successful life means gathering momentum upward, like the arrow that career workaholics visualize on money and power ladders.

What if Karen Armstrong's bliss, the study of theology,

had not been affirmed by the marketplace? It would not have detracted from her achievement of realizing her potentials. We need to get past those external marching orders "to make something" of ourselves, which I swear were issued to me in the hospital nursery. The bar needs not just to be lowered on what the "something" is; the bar needs to be blown to smithereens. It is indeed a product of Western thinking.

Mantra tip for death anxiety—My gain is my sister's gain; my brother's loss is my loss.

Another notion exists that success also is defined by singular moments that cast big auras. But not everyone goes for competitive gold, or wants to, or relates to the Olympic theme song's request for just one moment in time, or cares that Andy Warhol stretched it to allot each person a full 15 minutes in which to *matter*.

The difference, as perhaps Red Pollard knew, is whether that high is one moment or 15 minutes of recognized accomplishment, it does give us a leg up on esteem and how we feel about ourselves. Those who are fortunate to have them can cling to the memory of those special timeframes to buffer the darker moments when recriminations sneak in.

Wisdom is the only steady progression in life, besides wrinkles. Yet why, if wisdom is so wise, does gaining it so often bring resignation and regrets instead of motivation?

A remarkable coincidence occurred on the day after I addressed the anxiety relief that a death and rebirth of self-image would bring, no matter how late in life and no matter how much time had been frittered away or misdirected. I opened my *New York Times* to an article, "Low-Calorie-Diet Study Takes Scientists Aback."[3]

Scientists have long known that restricted diets can prolong life. However, they were not prepared for the startling findings that the life-extending effect kicks in within 48 hours, no matter how advanced in age the person might be, and continues as long, but only as long as the diet does. It is true the tests were with fruit flies, and scientists cannot confirm with certainty that this lesson holds with humans. But they do believe so!

Following that probability, Dr. Linda Partridge of University College in London said, "From the time a person starts on a restricted diet, they'll be like individuals of the same age who were always on that diet."[4] *The body contains no memory or damaging residue of bad habits from the past.* A person has to keep up with the new regimen or within the next two-day period will lose all positive life benefits, and the body will revert as though the person had never dieted at all.

However, in studies with mice, researchers found that a feast-famine routine on alternate days also produced prolongation of life similar to that of skinny mice who had been on the strict diet every day of their lives. Permanent damage, such as from a heart attack or detached retina, will not disappear; but implications are strong that it is the present alone that counts, not a crippling past legacy.

Do I agree that this study likely applies to the human and other species? Yes. Moreover, I suggest the principle holds for changes in attitude and perspective, too, for with the change, the past is erased, no longer a burden. Accepting that the correlation sticks also means no backsliding once on the path.

I was gratified to read these words of Daniel Callahan: "*How we die will be a function of the way we have lived our lives and the kind of person we have become.*"[5] Note Callahan did not write "the kind of person we were" or "the kind of person we have been." He used a verb of transformation.

Knowing that I will die as I have lived emotionally, I would certainly prefer to have evolved into a groove of positively, carelessly expending myself outwardly rather than negatively crawling through self-absorbed worries. The emotional goal is inner peace. Surely there is no greater spiritual achievement than inner peace at the finish line.

Meaning and Purpose in Life

Butler took aim at much the same angst, what Rosenthal called the fear of incompleteness, from this direction.
After one has lived a life of meaning, death may lose much of its terror. For what we fear most is not really death but a meaningless and absurd life. I believe most human beings can accept the basic fairness of each generation's taking its turn on the face of the planet if they are not cheated out of the full measure of their own turn.[6]

Both the Pulitzer Prize-winning gerontologist and the young leukemia victim were on the same page. *Getting the full measure of one's own turn refers to the ability of the true self to be activated to find meaningful direction.* Nothing more complicated than that.

"Realizing potentials" has nothing to do with achieving ego goals and everything to do with acting purposefully from a center of authentic feelings. Even if certain winning aptitudes are never recognized, if certain qualities like beauty and youth disappear, if career doors fail to open, if fixed dreams appear sacrificed, nothing has been lost, only reconfigured. The kaleidoscope has shifted and demands a change in vision.

James McCarthy, who has analyzed numerous studies, concludes *there is an intimate connection between overcoming death anxiety and depression and finding a purpose in life and consequent formation of an identity therein.* Also, both intrinsically and extrinsically religious people have a greater fear of death if they have a low purpose in life, but both are less afraid with a high sense of purpose.

Giving "the definition of intense death anxiety as *the fear of the loss of the self,"* McCarthy observes that its lifelong components, *the fears of abandonment and separation*, are core anxiety issues particularly heightened in the neurotic personality as well as in the vulnerable, weakened state of the terminally ill. Besides their direct relationship to lack of purpose and prolonged dissatisfaction with life, he also sees death anxiety and depression as root factors in defensive manic activity. Such manic activity is manifest in extreme preoccupation with work, athletics, possessions, social involvement, etc.[7]

Examples immediately come to mind in the work of Woody Allen. The filmmaker built his stable of movies around the struggles of unfulfilled characters, many neurotic, with this very same fear of incompleteness and lack of meaning.[8]

The irony is that placing meaningful value and purpose upon a personal journey does not necessarily infer that life carries meaning on its own. McCarthy and his peers write of a purpose in an individual life, and that is indeed a doable search and antidote to death anxiety. The reminder here is that this does not presuppose that in life each event fits neatly into the myth of higher meaning. Baumeister in *Meanings in Life* points out there may be no correct solutions to many moral dilemmas and choices, such as conflicting loyalties and the hotly debated moment when a fetus becomes a human being. To some questions, he states there may be "several answers and neither has precedence." Interestingly, Baumeister uses and defines "completeness" as "the assumption that everything makes sense...[that] there must be an answer....If completeness [by his definition] is indeed a myth, then there may be unsolvable problems." [9]

Death education lesson—Even if life intrinsically has no meaning, we still can consciously create and bring meaning into our own lives.

Against this specific philosophical backdrop some of the

most inspiring classics of world literature have set the dignity and value of the individual's struggle to find meaning for him or herself and the human community. In Albert Camus' *The Myth of Sisyphus*, the significance in a meaningless world is the individual's own *efforts and search* for meaning and fulfillment which give hope, majesty and *self-esteem* to a life.

Questions of meaning and absolutes have been around forever. A much thornier issue physically implodes our world and our Selves in the 21st century. Death-terror-management theorists posit that one's allegiance to a world view can bring anxiety relief if or when self-esteem is low. Enduring cultural and national ideologies defend against anxiety by giving its members a sense of stability, coherence and belonging to "a powerful entity greater than myself," Kastenbaum notes. What happens, he asks, if neither individual self-esteem nor cultural belief systems are adequate defense against death anxiety? *"What if the individual finds it more difficult to believe in traditional religious faiths and to embrace an uncritical patriotism?"*[10] In 2000, Kastenbaum's prescient thoughts were published, just prior to the events of 9/11.

World-view "faiths" have taken on ugly colors, belying coherence and stability, leaving many individuals either attached to black-and-white warmongering ideologies or adrift. A "Clash of the Titan Gods and Opposing Cultures" is the madness of our times. And it will likely not be resolved in our lifetimes.

How, then, to find individual meaning and purpose in life in this morass of horrific death and anxiety-heightening death symbols? Part of each of us, it seems, is wrenched away and caught up in the complicated grief and anxiety caused by sudden, catastrophic, mass homicides. Self-esteem seems almost an indulgent, selfish wish.

In Andre Malraux's *La Condition Humaine (Man's Fate)*, young Chinese Communist revolutionaries over 70 years ago invested their identification, meaning and lives in a cause for the betterment of peasants and workers. Acting on principles of higher meaning and benefit than the individual's is heroic *whether or not those absolutes exist*. Again, it is the value of personal efforts and investment for which the consensus is clear in relation to overcoming or lessening death anxiety. The irony and moral dilemma are the same for today's conflicting ideologies as they were 70 years ago for Malraux's. Heroic action is not necessarily right action, any more than might necessarily makes right.

Note the difference!

Far removed from the collective identification of those young Chinese revolutionaries and Eastern philosophies is the egocentric individualism in Western philosophies. The Self-negating tenets of Eastern principles and mysticism are incompatible with the Self-affirming ones of Occidental Man. Jung called the former "imagelessness." Paul Tillich called the latter "the courage to be." It is the Western courage-to-be culture to which these insights pertain, a culture in which the sun revolves around the self instead of vice versa. We are stuck with the cult of individual identity and achievement despite the fact that, "where preprogrammed lives are unthinkingly lived by those having minimal conceptions of identity, death is not problematic."[11]

The goal of having a real, individuated identity to which you have given meaning and self-esteem has only one drawback—intensified death anxiety when you confront its loss. How do we find a way to individuate lavishly till the curtain comes down and not be shaking in our boots?

Reality check—the detour to a purpose in life

In the past century of Western psychobabble and focus on the individual, few have spoken to their Western culture with greater clarity about the need to march to their own drum than

Otto Rank, Carl Jung and the equally ubiquitous Joseph Campbell. For Rank, each individual is unique and has the ability to create himself in unpredictable ways.[12] For Campbell, his famed hero's journey is one of separation, individuation and return. The self-knowledge gained on the journey hopefully includes knowledge of forks in the main road that can still lead to fulfillment. Indeed, that is the issue Jung addresses next, one which I believe bridges the gap between an idealized path and the reality of many life situations.

With the Western emphasis on individuation comes the warning that seeking and following one's authenticity can be a solitary road of inevitable mistakes. Jung cautioned that the sure and easier road is the road to avoid.

Getting personal—with a red flag

A fifteen-year-old girl asked Jung, "Professor, you are so clever. Could you please tell me the shortest path to my life's goal?"

Without a moment's hesitation Jung replied, "The detour." [13]

I agree with Jung, so much so that I would rewrite his second tombstone inscription (in Latin) which he also chose as the motto for his house: "Called or not called, the god will be there." I would state: "Called or not, the detour will be there." It is a cakewalk to accept some of these consensus insights if you are blind to the red flags called "circumstances" which can prevent putting them into practice. Most of us live the joke that life is what happens while we are making other plans. A satisfying purpose in life seldom turns out to fulfill a person's myopic definition of individuated bliss.

Whether chosen or imposed, whatever becomes our track *will* find us; but the opportunity to follow one's passions may not find us if we have interpreted them too rigidly and refuse to let the kaleidoscope rotate.

Consider this possibility when a door closes. *Consider that a change in perspective and self-investment in a life "out there," away from the narrow drives of the ego,* will relieve the problem which the success demands of American individualism presents in death anxiety. It is tough to accept any purpose in life that is not the one we would have chosen. The secret to inner peace at death is not having accepted resignation, but rather having created self-esteem and dignity in the detour.

"We regret to announce the following flights of bliss and aptitude have been cancelled due to circumstances beyond their control—or due to excess baggage."

- Mattie lost all track of time in writing poems and plays that brought her the high school Creative Writing prize. She got pregnant and had a baby instead of an abortion. She was delighted to get a boring assembly-line job that had daycare and great benefits. At home, raising the child and writing were hell on her nerves. Finally, after receiving 50 rejection letters from publishers, she decided she really had nothing to say after all.
- Mark had an 800 SAT score and a mentor-teacher who saw the IBM boardroom in his future. A scholarship to M.I.T. brought the first and last tears of joy he would know. Called home his freshman year when his only parent had a stroke, he went to work for a local hardware supplier and after hours became the primary caregiver at home. He married, and together he and his wife nursed his father and had three children. He became a regional inventory manager and an alcoholic.
- Luke was on his way up with the best data-entry job he could have dreamed of for himself at the World Trade Center. Later that day, he was brought out of the carnage, alive but blind, filled

with seeds of bitterness and hate; their crippling effects he had yet to feel.
- Joan made a tough decision never to marry and have children. Her higher bliss was to be a foreign correspondent in the Middle East. Early in her school career, she knew this was what she would excel and glory in, and that it wouldn't be fair to a family. She keeps a small petless, plantless apartment in Chicago, from which her widely syndicated column originates.

For those with strong career abilities and drives that frustrate them and goals unmet, Mattie, Mark and Luke are stereotypical scenarios. Only Joan succeeded in putting her primary source of bliss and purpose in life together.

The others did not choose but were given a purpose in life, detouring them from where their talents and bliss were headed. They may never embrace and make peace with the alternative. Then there may also be scenarios of paralyzing procrastination and self-doubts, frustrating any meeting of potentials with purposeful satisfaction. Whatever the psychological or circumstantial causes for self-defined failure and depression, the feeling that we have purposelessly wasted our time here heightens the fear of death.

Helen Thomas, White House bureau chief of United Press International, put Joan's and her own trade-off in this response to a question on the ingredients of happiness. "Love (a relationship) can make you happy if everything goes right. But you have less control over love than over what you make of yourself. In work maybe you have a better leverage on happiness in the sense of fulfilling who you are."[14] Compelling words for those with both favorable circumstances and early assessment of their special talents and bliss going for them.

Unfortunately, some people have neither the love relationship nor satisfying career option going for them. There are those, like an academic friend of mine, who bear sad testament to Butler's finding that people regret most what they did not do instead of what they did. My friend holds onto the memory of an exciting career offer in New York City, but one which had none of the guaranteed security of his tenured appointment. He turned it down because he had to support his wife and two small children and did not foresee she would leave him. In evaluating his past 70 years, his exact words were these: "I've done a couple of little things that were okay, but when I think of what I could have done instead....The world is filled with so much mediocrity and phoniness—to which I've added my share."

How many eulogies, including mine, did he say with those words? Unless, that is, we realize that those words and the stinging choice of "mediocrity" and "phoniness" are only the always-evaluating and -comparing Ego speaking, making us miserable again.

To all these people, Albert Schweitzer speaks eloquently. "Not one of us knows what effect his life produces, and what he gives to others; that is hidden from us and must remain so, though we are often allowed to see some little fraction of it, so that we may not lose courage....It is not always granted to the sower to live to see the harvest. All work that is worth anything is done in faith."[15]

Happily for many, many people their families are creative works-in-progress, and in their relationships is all the purpose in life they seek, one that meets their psychological needs. A menial job, losing a job or the lack of other fulfilling commitments have no comparable meaning. I suggest that it is because their focus is off themselves and on others.

What, then, awaits those who do not find total fulfillment in a love relationship and children—or, more likely, *have not had the opportunity to*, and many more who have not found purpose in work or other endeavors? Is there not another option which, by the doing, answers psychological needs?

There is. It does not repudiate Western culture's drive to individuate or the ability to act upon the potentials of the individual. What it repudiates is the ego's constant drive to put footlights and applause on the self above others. One dirty word consistently began to repeat in secular, thanatological insights regarding death anxiety. It is *ego*. "Lack of meaningful purpose" runs alongside in second place.

Letting go of ego and its replacement, identity with others, are the primary theistic and non-theistic teachings of Confucius, the Torah and especially of the Buddha and Jesus. They all stress that *compassionate identity with others* is the best lesson to living a satisfying life and brings the sense of completeness that will stand *anyone* in good stead during the body's terminal days. The consensus of secular death educators and that of the founders of major spiritual traditions turned out to be identical, even though one was based on clinical studies and the other on moral precepts. When all roads in research lead to Rome, Rome it is, not Detroit.

Consequently, no matter how simplistic and saccharin the wrapping, this option is offered with confidence: When personal and professional daily living seem bereft of sustained, fulfilling direction, the *conscious* treatment of others in one's dealings and judgments will prove a significant calling and purpose in life.

Proof that this is no first-grade, Sunday-School suggestion lies in the Holocaust, the My Lai Massacres and the Iraqi prisoner-abuse scandal. Behavioral psychologists agree that such group atrocities have two reasons in common: blind obedience to authority and the inability to see the victims as fellow humans.

What were the Nuremberg trials all about if not the moral responsibility of individual conscience to stand up to any authority which dehumanizes others? Hitler, Jim Jones of the Guyana tragedy and Saddam are the worst of *ego* acting and separating one identity from others. Conscience is the best of the *authentic self* reacting. Matters of conscience, as tested in the above examples, are where individualism should have functioned best but failed to do so. Thus, becoming role models in the treatment of others and identity with them is giving the world what it needs most in this hostile, nuclear age.

It is no small purpose in life to adopt. Such a calling is an opportunity to make an innovative imprint. "There is a passage in the story of the Holy Grail which says that a Knight must enter the forest at a place that he himself has chosen. If he simply follows an established path, going in someone else's footsteps, then he won't have an adventure."[16]

Creative avenues of outreach and relationship abound. Daily mindful practice applies a consistent attitude instead of afterthought tokenism (of which frequently I am guilty). Due to misconceptions and prejudgment, my personal resistance has been to the homeless. The streets are filled with people in pain. Generic profiling misses and dehumanizes the singular story and value each "street person" holds, to which I can connect.

This means of traveling, prudently yet with indiscriminate empathy, conveys in words and acts that fellow sentient beings on this planet are equally one's brothers and sisters. Censured are those prejudiced or self-righteous stands that poison polity and speech. Disavowed, and surely godless, are any divisive claims of religious fundamentalism—"theirs" and "ours."

Moving beyond ego into identity with endless faces and journeys in the world is what Simmons and others call breaking through to "big mind." The illusion of separateness vanishes.

If you want a solution, in lock step with consensus insights, to the search for substantive life purpose that will transcend death anxiety and bring inner peace to your last days, you have it.

As the revolutionary Jesus would point out, that answer is right in front of us, and we don't see it.

---

[1] Hillenbrand, Laura. *Seabiscuit: An American Legend.* New York: Random House, 2001. Illustrated Ed., 2003, p. 20.
[2] PBS Home Video. *American Experience: Seabiscuit.* Boston: WGBH-TV, 2003.
[3] Kolata, Gina. "Low-Calorie-Diet Study Takes Scientists Aback." *The New York Times.* 19 September 2003: A16.
[4] Editorial. "News to Chew Over: Eat Better and Live Longer." *Austin [TX] American-Statesman.* 21 September 2003.
[5] Callahan, Daniel. Foreword. Robert E. Kavanaugh. *Facing Death.* Los Angeles: Nash, 1972, p. xii.
[6] Butler, Robert N., M.D. *Why Survive? Being Old in America.* New York: Harper & Row, 1975, p. 422.
[7] McCarthy, James B. *Death Anxiety: The Loss of the Self.* New York: Gardner, 1980.
[8] Lee, Sander H. *Woody Allen's Angst: Philosophical Commentaries on His Serious Films.* Jefferson, NC, & London: McFarland & Co., Inc., 1997.
[9] Baumeister, Roy F. *Meanings in Life.* New York: The Guilford Press, 1991, pp. 63-64.
[10] Kastenbaum, Robert J., Ph.D. *The Psychology of Death.* 3rd Ed. New York: Springer, 2000, pp. 139-140.
[11] Kearl, Michael C. *Endings: A Sociology of Death and Dying.* New York & Oxford: Oxford University Press, 1989, p. 34.
[12] Lieberman, E. James, M.D. *Acts of Will: The Life and Work of Otto Rank.* New York: Free Press, 1985.
[13] Stern, Paul. *C. G. Jung: The Haunted Prophet.* New York: George Braziller, 1976, pp. 189-90.
[14] Wholey, Dennis. *Are You Happy?* Boston: Houghton-Mifflin, 1986, p. 104.
[15] Schweitzer, Albert. *Memories of Childhood and Youth.* New York: Macmillan, 1955, pp. 68, 77.
[16] Armstrong, Karen. Presentations. "Some Tips from the Axial Age" and "The Spiral Staircase." Westar Institute Spring Meeting. New York, 4-6 March 2004.

Chapter 5

Moving Outside the Frame

> *It is not that the person who eschews organized religion is bereft; it is that the person who lacks some stabilizing beliefs—even (or especially) in oneself—is lost....[When one is dying] what seems to be important is not so much the content of any philosophy of life, religion or creed, as how firmly, easily, and comfortably that belief is held...the internal comfort which that belief system gives to that person.*
> —Edwin Shneidman[1]

> *Whatever your heart clings to and confides in, that is really your God.*
> —Martin Luther

Both quotes are about authenticity and commitment. I believe Luther's metaphoric language describes God as whatever the lighthouse is that guides the authentic self.

This chapter takes a final look at tensions between the ego and authentic self, and between individualism and shared identity. It will reconcile them in a single directive for what works best to overcome and move outside the crippling constraint of death anxiety.

The difference between ego and self-esteem

It is the tension between self-realization and ego interests that I found so problematic in death education. Specifically, self-esteem and ego are opposing forces in the field of death education and sticky allies in the Western cult of the individual.

I think of it this way. The real self is revealed in authentic feelings and the spontaneous acts and commitments which are born in them.

Quite separately, the ego tries to take that identity and make something of it that is superior and separate from others. The ego fears losing its specialness in death.

Here is where I place a third element—conscience. It is a human leveler. It taps a shared reservoir of embedded ethical and cultural values, and among these the authentic self chooses its place and voice. Lasting self-esteem is based on following conscience, not ego. If self-esteem is thought of in this way, as based on following conscience, and ego as based on a show-off persona, the two can easily be separated. And separated they must be, because ego heightens death anxiety, while self-esteem lessens it.

The problem of American individualism

Is it not narcissistic and peculiarly Western to be self-absorbed in realizing one's own potentials, not the community's or the group's? The individual hopes for more meaning to life than paying taxes, and being an adequate family person, and having an "exercise in paperwork as a career," Baumeister writes. He argues that modern times have brought uncertainty about the meaning of life and basic values, which particularly heightens the discomfort of death.

The response has been "to elevate selfhood and the cultivation of identity into basic, compelling values" unlike our forebears and Eastern cultures who still today are supported by community values that would survive them. "If we rely on the quest for identity and self-knowledge to give life meaning, we make ourselves vulnerable to death in an almost unprecedented way....Death takes away not only our life but also what gave it value....The high value that people today place on self and identity is a mixed blessing. It helps fill the value gap and allows people to make judgments about what is good and bad, right and wrong, despite modern society's inability to agree on broad universal morals. It leaves people naked in the face of death. It is a value that fails people at one of the times when they need it the most."[2]

However, Kearl states that in the U.S. "this threat to meaningfulness is countered by continuing beliefs in an afterlife—particularly for the most educated."[3]

Regarding the extent of America's replacement of afterlife certainty for the problem of death anxiety that individualism causes, he cites the International Social Survey Program on religion in 17 nations: "With 55 per cent definitely believing and nearly 80 per cent thinking it at least probable, Americans are the least likely to harbor any doubts about a post-mortem existence, even when compared with several strongly Catholic nations....Americans are most likely to strongly agree that 'there is a God who concerns himself with every human being personally' and the most likely to disagree with the statement 'In my opinion, life does not serve any purpose'." (This 1991 response to the question of no meaning in life ranged from 89% in Russia to 8% in the U.S.)

Here is where it gets even more interesting. Kearl cites the combined General Social Surveys from 1973 to 1994 conducted by the National Opinion Research Center. The findings show in the U.S. "belief in life after death actually increases with education, regardless of the level of religiosity," among fundamentalist and moderate Protestants and Catholics. Americans are more than 25% "more likely than the British and New Zealanders to believe in Heaven *and more than twice as likely to believe in Hell.*" Here, for me, is the corker: "*Nearly two-thirds of Americans agree, 'You have to take care of yourself first, and if you have any energy left over, then help other people'.*"[4]

To draw some conclusions: American individualism has not been Mother's Little Helper in facing death. Happily, the problem has been assuaged for maybe half of us by a firm belief in an afterlife. This belief should provide meaningfulness similar to that known by collective societies and our ancestors whose values would outlive the individual. This, in turn, provides a defense against vulnerability to death and its anxiety.

Unhappily, as the number who believe in hell is also great, we are left with many variables that cloud an easy correlation between a belief in an afterlife and lessened death anxiety. Other polls show a large number of Americans believe they will go to heaven and lead to the conclusion that afterlife certainty is a good buffer against death anxiety for many Americans and a good counterpoint to the problem of individualism. But not for everyone.

This raises the following questions. How, then, can we respond to the peculiar American problem of narcissistic fulfillment and vulnerability to heightened death anxiety, unknown in cultures of collective identity and value systems? How can we reconcile in American terms the unique intensity of death fears peculiar to a self-involved Western culture, short of rebirth in Japan or India? How can we move to a more comfortable position if some of us are stuck with individualism's characteristic fears of dying incomplete or without significance?

This dilemma screams to be noticed in all the issues raised in these first chapters, and in their search for an American-friendly resolution. I suggested the American version of the Eastern collective perspective in the last chapter and propose it again here.

Looking anew at the fear of incompleteness of one's life, what can be said about death anxiety kindled by regrets of unfulfilled individual potentials and plans? How do we reconcile the other fear, of extinction without significance, in our Western culture which glorifies individual achievement? It could be said that the former has to do really with how we feel about ourselves, and the latter has to do with how posterity feels about us. But that is wrong. Both have to do with how we perceive ourselves.

A life review, such as in the D-Day exercise, can change your perspective on your past, uncover the threads or direction of a purpose in life and thereby change your self-concept. Elevating self-esteem, *however* it occurs, will be enough defense for some. Certainly, it is a terrific place to start.

I have spent years now working with the insights of the past four chapters which comprise Part I as they emerged as single threads through the texts of my research. They began to fall together into the same pile, same direction.

William James nailed the entry code to the pile's contents when he wrote, "The greatest discovery of my generation is *that a human being can change his life by changing his attitude of mind.*" I have come to realize that simply *by changing perspective*, one's life can end like a Japanese drawing—somewhere outside the frame. Further, those fears of unrealized potentials, an inauthentic life and extinction without significance—which can be such crippling components of death anxiety—will be overcome.

This change of perspective is a death-and-rebirth experience. *All that is required to move outside the frame is to move outside the ego.* The rest—the fears of not having enough time, of seldom doing it right, of leaving no stain upon the silence that says you mattered—will disappear. Along with the ego, they will be literally out of focus because the focus will be elsewhere. There is no loss of identity, only a changed one, from self to Self amid the Big Mind we all share.

The investment opportunities for meaningful purpose

extend beyond compassion and identity with others. Robert E. Kavanaugh, a former Roman Catholic priest turned provost and professor at UC/San Diego, words the consensus and most powerful prescription of all for death anxiety: "It is not the content of a man's creed that makes him confident and peaceful near life's brink. It is more the quality of his art of believing that counts. Faith is simply *that total commitment of the entire person to an ideal, a way of life, a set of values, to anything or anyone beyond the narrow limitations of myself: God, mankind, the poor, science, human relations, growth and development, anything capable of bringing meaning and purpose to life.* True believers are those who internalize and live what they claim to believe. This quality of believing *is any man's major asset in facing his own death.*"[5]

All the insights in my research regarding the psychological fears of death come together in Dr. Kavanaugh's words. Adding the problem of individualism and the ego, a fair statement might be this. *If* we can activate the true self in a meaningful way to do its own thing, yet forswear the ego's insidious plans and constant efforts to make the Self feel special and separate from others, *then* we have brought the best anxiety medicine of the Eastern perspective to Western individualism. *To lose the ego in an external commitment*—be it to one's children, a musical composition, or *some higher end benefit to others* from one's professional or personal time—*will serve anyone well in facing death.*

Karen Armstrong found what can only be called a "watershed footnote" at a page bottom of Volume One of Marshall G.S. Hodgson's *The Venture of Islam*. Hodgson cautions the scholar of religion not to proceed from a post-enlightenment, patronizing position. Rather the scholar should wait until he has digested the full context of his subject's own conventions and perspective. Continue to ask "but why?" until he or she can feel an "immediate, human grasp...[and] himself doing the same thing." This method of writing is one of compassion, Armstrong notes, which means "feeling with" her subject. This was an essential step while writing *Muhammad*, she adds, requiring what Saint Paul "had called a *kenosis*, an emptying of self." In identifying with the emotions and circumstances of her subject, Armstrong's "I" had to recede.

In its place, while writing, she encountered moments of ecstasy, awe and transcendence.[6] Were these moments not similar to what Philip Simmons felt when he sensed himself playing through the children at the piano recital? Such moments are portals, surely, to Big Mind, known as God by some. When they occur, time stands still. These flickers of recognition and transcendence are very much outside the frame of our small existence.

James left another quotable quote that trumps the others in brevity and almost does so in truth: "The greatest use of life is to spend it on something that will outlast it." The problem is any implication that the "something" must have a sticking post-self stamp on it. I believe these death educators and past sages mean an uncalculated spinning outward of energy into the world, without prejudging what retention one's actions will have in memory.

Don Cupitt calls this *solar living* and *solar ethics*. A Fellow and former Dean of Emmanuel College, Cambridge, he has authored over 30 books. Frequently, he lectures on the philosophy of religion and ethics and offers this concept as a means of religious living where conviction of an immortal soul and heavenly world do not exist. Cupitt believes Christianity in England is close to free fall.

Using oneself up like the sun is a replacement ethic he offers for a satisfying life and its conclusion. "We obtain such life satisfaction as we can get by all the time pouring ourselves out into symbolic expression." The self "lives by dying all the time, so that the harder we live, the more death disappears as any kind of problem. Solar living is eternal life: it overcomes the traditional polarity of life and death."[7]

Noting that solarity is careless and spendthrift, Cupitt writes that the solar ethic is one of "self-outing, self-outpouring, self-shedding. We are no longer fearful about dying, or afraid to give ourselves away. We can get ourselves together only by leaving ourselves behind. That is solarity—to live by dying all the time, heedless like the sun and in the spirit of the Sermon on the Mount. Solar ethics is a radically emotivist and expressionist reading of the ethics of Jesus."[8]

Cupitt's sun metaphor and Simmons' concept of "big mind," which I prefer to capitalize in likeness to God, are both outwardly committed visual perspectives. The phrasing and examples used here around them and other concepts may occasionally recall inspirational platitudes spilling out of "Be All You Can Be" bookstore sections. Solar living, for example, could aptly cop and run under the slogan "Go for the Burn!" Such a connection is fun and a great memory aid. Popularizing heavy material makes it easily accessible.

But doing so should never put at peril or dumb down the integrity, intentions and no-nonsense conclusions of these Western research scholars and eminent educators. With this responsibility, I choose my favorite catch phrase and coping tool, that of Big Mind, which is an exquisite metaphysical fit with the consensus bottom line, to conclude this section.

In moving outwardly beyond the narrow limitations of our egos to collective concerns, our perspective becomes collective. I suggest that this path into Big Mind, or universal soul, has the same goalpost as Jesus' commandments to love your neighbor as yourself and your enemy likewise. It is blind to religious labels.

This path is through the same response of compassion which is the Buddhist's sole focus of activism. It is the path for those who do not find or have families, much less careers, as adequate defense against death anxiety and specific death fears. It is the genus of spontaneity and authenticity, the goal of meditation and, for some, God. It is the way out for individualism's unique fears of failure and post-self insignificance. This mental realm beyond the ego is the womb of inspiration and belongs to the artist type's creative process. One metaphysical viewpoint sees this state of mind as the home of perfect love which casts out all fear.

Big Mind is limitless and deathless. Moving into its perspective is moving outside the frame, namely, transcending the fear of dying and its power over us. The journey can begin right now from self to Self, into identity with Big Mind. In this journey we learn and practice the lesson of the Universe taught by Lao-tzu. "The reason why the universe is eternal is that it does not live for itself; it gives life to others as it transforms."

---

[1] Shneidman, Edwin. *Voices of Death*. New York: Harper & Row, 1980, p. 190.
[2] Baumeister, Roy F. *Meanings of Life*. New York: Guilford Press, 1991, pp. 5-6.
[3] Kearl, Michael. "You Never Have to Die." *The Unknown Country: Death in Australia, Britain and the USA*. Kathy Charmaz, Glennys Howarth and Allan Kellehear, eds. New York: St. Martin's Press, 1997, p. 192.
[4] Ibid., pp. 186-193.
[5] Kavanaugh, Robert E. *Facing Death*. Los Angeles: Nash, 1972, pp. 222-23. (emphasis mine)
[6] Armstrong, Karen. *The Spiral Staircase: My Climb out of Darkness*. New York & Toronto: Knopf, 2004, pp. 289-290.
[7] Cupitt, Don. *Emptiness and Brightness*. Santa Rosa, CA: Polebridge Press, 2001, pp. 51-52.
[8] —. *After God: The Future of Religion*. New York: Basic Books, 1997, pp. 90, 125.

PART II

LOSS OF THE PHYSICAL SELF

The fears of pain, dependency and the loss of control

People are like stained glass windows. The true beauty can be seen only when there is light from within. The darker the night, the brighter the windows.
—Elisabeth Kubler-Ross[1]

PART II confronts the fears in the physical process of letting go.

Chapter 6

Let Go and Let Who?

The most overwhelming pains we experience are the result of a desperate attempt to grasp something too tightly. Part I looked at letting go psychologically and emotionally. Part II previews the fears about the last stage—when a terminal diagnosis has been confirmed, when the loss of the self is finally imminent and we have to let go physically.

Remember that guy climbing the mountain, negotiating with God? He is trying to bargain his way out of letting go. God tells him to trust Him and let go. Terrified, the man yells back, "Anyone else up there?"

Stunningly, in the first half of the 20th century, God's power, death and that answer changed, and in just the last 50 years have begun to change again.

Geoffrey Gorer was the British anthropologist who, in his 1965 book *Death, Grief, and Mourning*, which includes his famous 1955 article "The Pornography of Death," notes the changes in British death attitudes which he attributes primarily to World War I. Gone were the ritual black clothing and crepe hanging in tribute. Gone were communal grieving and spiritual enthronement of Dickens' Little Nell. It was not appropriate to wallow in ostentatious grief at a time calling for stiff upper lips.

Gorer writes, "In the twentieth century, however, there seems to have been an unremarked shift in prudery; whereas copulation has become more and more 'mentionable,' particularly in the Angle-Saxon societies, death has become more and more 'unmentionable' as a *natural process*."

Thus, the early Victorian openness toward natural death, spiritualized and hallowed, prudishly went into hiding starting at the turn of the century while sex, its sensations rather than its emotions, began to come out of the closet. Violent, unnatural death took the stage, from shoot 'em ups and thrillers to war and spy stories. Here is Gorer's grand plea, made in 1955: "If we dislike the modern pornography of death, then we must give back to death—natural death—its parade and publicity, re-admit grief and mourning. If we make death unmentionable in polite society—'not before the children'—we almost ensure the continuation of the 'horror comic'."[2]

The provocative and respected French historian Philippe Aries decried likewise what he called "forbidden death." Lonely hospital deaths embedded in shame and secrecy reflected the developing Western attitudes around 1930-1950. Aries contended that in every age, how a society approached death reflected how they led life.[3]

Writing more recently, Robert Wells in *Facing the "King of Terrors"* takes a contrarian view to Gorer on such causal points as the war factor. His study of changes in death attitudes and perceptions in Schenectady, New York, 1750 to 1990, led him to conclude that the shift was the outcome of the changes within the community itself, from shared rituals and traditional, small-town customs to ethnic diversity and mechanistic systems. Regarding the attitudinal change, Wells writes, "By the 20th century, to prepare was to vaccinate and filter water, not to ready one's soul for an unpredictable call." He agrees with others that we have lost many of the symbols and vocabulary to give death meaning.[4]

In his presentation "Death as a Cultural Phenomenon,"[5] Alan Friedman reflects on Gorer's conclusions that those certainties disappeared with The Great War. It and its successor war resulted in bodies unceremoniously and even unidentifiably strewn *en masse* across fields. In England, The Great Flu

Epidemic of 1917-18 was also emphatically devastating and desensitizing. In tandem with this shift in attitudes on both sides of the Atlantic, doctors displaced women in death and childbirth. Death moved from God's hands to those of the medical community. The deathbed moved from the home and the family's bosom to hospitals and nursing facilities.

Ballpark statistics on American deaths in 1900 indicate 80% took place in the home. Heading into the 1980s, 70-80% were estimated occurring in institutions.

Norbert Elias in *The Loneliness of the Dying* scrutinizes the more developed societies and chillingly writes, "*Never before have people died so noiselessly and hygienically as today in these societies, and never in social conditions so much fostering solitude.*"[6] Such deserts of loneliness foster anxiety and the specific fear and despair of dependency, strange surroundings and tubes.

No wonder Shneidman's often-cited major survey in *Psychology Today* in 1970 reported the preferred choice of death to be "Sudden, but not violent death"—38%! "Quiet, dignified death" only pulled 30%! What an indictment of what had occurred so quickly and insidiously! *The Book of Common Prayer* (1559) had sent a strong warning, "*...and from sudden death Good Lord deliver us.*" Just 400 years later in America, sudden death is the winning choice—by a significant 8% margin! "Spare us from sudden death" became "spare us from sterile, heroic measures" and the denial of death by anxiety-ridden doctors[7] who see it as professional failure.

There have been good reasons to fear not death but the process of dying in the past century. In too many cases modern technology lacked a heart. If that poor climber was clinging in fear to his branch during this long time, he may have changed his tune. He may have learned a greater fear of *not* being allowed to die by the Replacement Decision-makers, no matter how tired and ready his body and soul are.

Stonewalling and denial are not unique to the medical community. Although a compassionate effort was made to keep them at home, my grandparents were told, as they died in the 1960s, that they were going to be okay. My parents never told them they were dying. That is robbery.

Softly in the '50s and '60s wonderful countering currents started moving. These currents had names. Dame Cecily Saunders in Britain started St. Christopher's Hospice. A pint-sized, Swiss, female doctor, Elisabeth Kubler-Ross came to a Chicago hospital and shook the medical establishment's ground by starting open, unflinching dialogue with terminal patients, thus providing them a language for dying. She and a new breed of thanatologists like Herman Feifel pronounced technology avoided rather than supported the reality of death. When in 1974 the first hospice home services arrived in the United States, its sole focus was palliative (pain-preventive) care and patient autonomy. By 1994, 2000 hospices dotted this country.

I particularly like Richard Kalish's imagery in explaining the situation to which this major confluence was responding. In 1980 Kalish looked at the shift during the preceding part of the 20th century and commented, "The ultimate concern is no longer that of heavenly immortality, but of a long and healthy life on earth, perhaps even of earthly immortality. In that case the priesthood must change. When the god is secular, the priesthood must also be secular."[8] In the switch from priest to physician, Kalish quoted Sam Keen, "Disease has replaced sin as the condition from which to be saved." However, then, Kalish continued, longevity was found to be wanting by many for whom it merely translated into thoughts of loneliness, lingering in nursing homes and deteriorating bodies submitted to impersonal x-ray machines and technicians.

So it was in the United States that the hospice principles found fertile root, and the death educators whose names appear here throughout became a deaconship of sorts. This new field lacked the power of both priesthoods, cleric and medical, since its work involved neither long life nor continued life after death. Rather these educators functioned then and continue to do so now as facilitators promoting appropriate deaths and enhancing quality of life through preparation for and acceptance of death.

Now, as we have moved forward into the 21st century, a meeting of minds has occurred. Three heretofore disjointed supports—1) the human emotional, 2) the spiritual/religious and 3) the medical—have been synthesized into a whole delivery response system. Critically, the dying person has been handed back the steering wheel so that the control through this final period is his or hers to navigate. Viewed from within an advanced Western culture, particularly by an American with Medicare's hospice benefit, *at no other point in history have so many of our fears of death—our psychological and bodily anxieties—been addressed and given either guidance or solutions.* Personally, I am not sure that this is a great time to live because of the polarized hatred in the world. But I know this is a great time to die.

A recent challenge remains, however. It is the epidemic of AIDS. Calling it a meaning-laden disease, Friedman says, "AIDS narratives—proclaiming the pain, and outrage, and tragedy of individual experiences; refuting medical technology's promises of a better life—have been marginalized by a society conflicted over whether to deny death or sex or the relationship between them." [9] To this I would add an additional red challenge flag for others who die alone and/or who are also marginalized by society.

Symbols and rituals

We have only to look back to the 13th century in Western Europe to see how death was once an event of highest ritual.

There was even a particular horizontal dying position, called "gisant" in French. There, according to Aries, the dying person ceremoniously took leave of others, both giving and receiving absolution, and awaited death with little emotion.[10]

All who addressed the issue agreed on the need to reinstate old symbols or invent new ones and vocabulary to honor and give meaning to an individual life's conclusion.

In *On Our Way*, Kastenbaum points out that ritual, unlike routine, usually involves magic, faith, transformation and an occasion beyond one's self. Ritual also re-enacts intense emotions and events deeply embedded and recalled to therapeutic efficacy. These elements are critical, he reminds, in that many oppressed in the world have *only* ritual and faith and no other palliative resources to turn to in stressful and terminal situations.[11]

This worthy criticism is from a New Zealander: "Many of the secular funerals and weddings and naming ceremonies I've experienced have been put together carefully and tastefully and have undoubtedly respected the wishes of the principal participants, but I sometimes feel they lack muscle—they're *pretty rather than powerful*. Do they reach into the depths and brush their fingertips against the heights?"

The writer, Jill Harris, says the rituals of Christian faith, with its transforming potential and theme of liberation, move her. But she left the church, feeling it ignored the "sea-change in world view which has caused millions of people to leave. Little in its rituals makes any concession to this huge cultural shift which, after all, has been happening for 400 years."[12]

There is much to learn and rebuild from the rituals and customs maintained in certain pockets of the United States. In particular, many of the religious dying and death attitudes and cultural traditions of Native Americans form a remarkable, real-life mirror of the great majority of the consensus prescriptions that I found in my research.

There is great cultural diversity in this regard among the 350 different tribes in the United States. By way of example, the Apache consider the dead body to be a shell that has been emptied, whereas the Lakota regard the body as sacred and communicate with it, rejecting autopsies and cremation. The Navajo, unlike most of the tribes, do not believe in an afterlife. Looking closer at the large Lakota nation's customs in dying, Dr. Martin Brokenleg explains that actual specifics of a certain afterlife for humans and animals in Spirit Land hold little curiosity, nor does the continuous, *cyclical* nature of life and death hold fear. The pre-existing soul leaves some token of its presence behind when it goes on to its assured afterlife.

No Lakota wants to die alone, and other members feel guilt if this occurs. Moreover, they want to return to their reservation for burial, no matter their place of residence at the moment of death. Among Lakota customs Brokenleg notes that no intoxicants are used from the moment of death until after burial, although tobacco smoking is a long-honored tradition. Sacred funeral rites, emotionally expressive memorial ceremonies, tribal songs and drums, a three-day lying-in-state and traditional tributary meals punctuate a year of mourning.

A family means the extended family, and death education for children is early and natural by participation in customs with their elders. Because family, not material possessions, has importance, the deceased's and other family possessions are burned or communally distributed. The cycle is symbolically completed in such divestiture, life's values and purpose reinforced, the family newly defined without the deceased's physical presence.[13]

Irish notes that, as with many of these special cultural pockets in the United States, adaptations are needed, such as hospital accommodation for large numbers of relatives, a (less-frequent) request for a medicine man instead of a Christian cleric and for the possibility of sage being burned.

Many of these memorial customs I would wish for myself, not to mention sage has a delightful smell. However, I am not going to race quite yet to any of them, warbling, "I'm an Indian, too." The reality of today, says Irish, is that "almost all Native Americans face harsh conditions on reservations and in urban life: high unemployment, considerable alcoholism, poor health, high suicide rates, and frequent despair. None of these conditions characterized their traditional vigorous, creative and sustainable lives."[14]

The American culture struggles against death more than many others. It has seemed like letting go has almost been treated as an option. The way Arnold Toynbee put it, "Death is un-American."[15] However, as Irish has pointed out, there are noteworthy ethnic exceptions. During past decades "real death" has been relatively unknown to much of middle-class, white, suburban America; whereas children on Indian reservations, Hispanics, rural Southern blacks and urban ghetto communities confront death directly and intimately. Mexican-Americans have deeply embedded Catholic rituals surrounding rites of passage. Theirs is a firm belief in God's will being done and in an afterlife that softens the acceptance of death. Their culture reflects a fatalistic view that death is an ever-present reality for which one must be ever ready.

African Americans are similarly more in rhythm with dying. Whereas Whites are stoic and subdued in their grieving and funeral customs, Blacks are passionate and communal in emotion and gospel song. Irish notes about 90% of church-affiliated Blacks are Protestant, with the far greater population percentage in the South. Families are more extended in the South and nuclear in the North where support systems and time may be smaller and shorter. In what Irish calls an "explosion" over the last approximately fifteen years, violent deaths in gang, domestic and drug situations among teenage black youth have been horrific.[16] I have heard repeatedly over the years speakers focus on certain urban areas where children were unable to assume that they would live to be 20. Living with similar anticipation and apprehension, fellow children die in many countries today. Theirs has been a fear of dying for which I have no words.

Of course, the world's poverty-stricken always have accepted and treated death familiarly, with a great deal of fatal resignation. Besides culture, poverty is a sister environment when it comes to the ability to let go.

Who better has shown the relationship of a person's socio-economic status to death acceptance than Tolstoy in *Master and Man*? The peasant Nikita waits stoically in the blizzard for death to come, accepting the process with the hope that in dying God will release him from the hardships of this life. Beside him, his mercenary master, the merchant Vasili, tries to fight nature in order to get to a sale on time. He has something to live for, namely a life "worth" something, and Nikita does not.

It is a powerful tale.

---

[1] Gill, Derek. *Quest: The Life of Elisabeth Kubler-Ross.* New York: Harper & Row, 1980, p. 316.
[2] Gorer, Geoffrey. "The Pornography of Death." *Encounter.* October 1955. As reprinted in Gorer. *Death, Grief, and Mourning.* New York: Doubleday, 1965.
[3] Aries, Philippe. *Western Attitudes Toward Death: From the Middle Ages to the Present.* Baltimore & London: John Hopkins University Press, 1974.
[4] Wells, Robert V. *Facing the "King of Terrors": Death and Society in an American Community, 1750-1990.* Cambridge: Cambridge University Press, 2000, pp. 283-88. Quote, p. 285.
[5] Friedman, Alan. Presentation. "Death as a Cultural Phenomenon." Humanities Research Center, The University of Texas at Austin. 6 November 2003.

[6] Elias, Norbert. *The Loneliness of the Dying.* Oxford: Basil Blackwell, 1985, p. 85.

[7] Schulz, Richard, and David Aderman. "Physicians' Death Anxiety and Patient Outcomes." *Omega: Journal of Death and Dying.* Robert J. Kastenbaum, Ph.D., ed. 9.4 (1978-79): 299-319. Survey found that patients of doctors who had a high death anxiety when admitted to final hospitalization remained in the hospital an average of five days longer before dying than patients of doctors of medium and low death anxiety. They speculate that either these physicians were more likely to use heroic measures to prolong life or they admitted patients earlier.

[8] Kalish, Richard A. "Death Educator as Deacon." *Omega: Journal of Death and Dying.* Robert J. Kastenbaum, Ph.D., ed. Farmingdale, NY: Baywood. 11.1 (1980-81): 73-83.

[9] Freidman. Op. cit.

[10] Aries. Op. cit., pp. 8-13.

[11] Kastenbaum, Robert J., Ph.D. *On Our Way: The Final Passage Through Life and Death.* Berkeley & Los Angeles: University of California Press, 2004.

[12] Harris, Jill. "Religious Ritual for a Secular Society." *Sea of Faith.* Loughborough, UK: Sea of Faith Network. 63: 10 January 2004. (emphasis mine)

[13] Brokenleg, Martin, and David Middleton. "Native Americans: Adapting, Yet Retaining." *Ethnic Variations in Dying, Death, and Grief: Diversity in Universality.* Donald P. Irish, Kathleen F. Lundquist and Vivian Jenkins Nelson, eds. Washington, D.C.: Taylor & Francis, 1993, pp. 103-12.

[14] Irish, Donald P. "Diversity in Universality: Dying, Death and Grief." Kathy Charmaz, Glennys Howarth and Allan Kellehear, eds. *The Unknown Country: Death in Australia, Britain and the USA.* New York: St. Martin's Press, 1997, pp. 250-51.

[15] Toynbee, Arnold. "Changing Attitudes Toward Death in the Modern Western World." Arnold Toynbee, et al. *Man's Concern with Death.* New York: McGraw-Hill, 1969.

[16] Irish. Op. cit., pp. 242-56.

CHAPTER 7

COPING

A Personal Role Model

William James described Sarah Bernhardt as one who came into the world with a magnum of champagne to her credit. It can be reasonably presumed she also had all the esteem and sense of fulfilled potentials in life so as to have inner peace on her way out of it in 1923.

First, the illegitimate daughter of a French courtesan. Next, a child given to adoring nuns to educate. Then, a young woman escaping to the morals and morass of the decadent theatre world. She thrived, using men, talent and fame to achieve mercenary goals and a materialistic lifestyle of opulence. Indeed, she ate cake while the populace starved.

You can say that, *or* you can say: Here was a girl with little going for her. Born of one of her mother's keepers, an obstacle to her mother's profession, shunted to a convent, she yearned to be a nun and remain safe and selfless. Instead, she took the course suggested by a maternal suitor, one who may have fondled her as others perhaps had, and auditioned for the theatre and a life that could support an aging mother when the men and their money dwindled accordingly. Extravagant in taste. Extravagant in generosity.

Here was a girl, born 100 years exactly before me, a woman whose initials match my own. Whose number of biographers approaches the profusion saved for Jesus, and about whose life and talent they could uncover almost as little ill, save excess. Whose multi-faceted creativity shone on all fronts, from sculpture to painting to writing to roles she immortalized. Such genius usually carries the curse of some madness and anguish. Hers did not. Her mind and memory remained faithful and focused to her last breath.

Such excess brings the gods and their wrath. She foiled them. When her leg was amputated at age seventy-two, she wired friends, "My leg cut off tomorrow. I'm so happy." To stricken companions, as she was rolled to the operating room, she mustered, "Allons, enfants! Un peu de courage!" and a few bars of "La Marseillaise."

She was, from start to finish, a warrior to setbacks that would have kept anyone else down for the count. I found her on a list of actors who were also authors. From the first, she was contagious.

Go on. Embellish me. You can't, you know, *she taunts.*

She's right. I laughed aloud, which in itself is a rare joy. It's impossible to exaggerate her excesses or her creativity.

Above all, her laughter held the reins of her life. It was the shimmering tablecloth on which she feasted every day of her life. The source of her laughter was indeed the well that sustained her through the pain and loss of a leg that would have silenced the humor and vision of anyone other than The Divine Sarah.

Shared lifelines of creativity and humor make us soulmates. Our cultural backgrounds and career experiences account for our differences. Also, fierce determination and opportune timing. Both were there for her when needed.

A personality so clearly defined and documented that death was no barrier to her spirit, her persona leaps from the pages and photos intact and remains suspended to this day. In her resided the authentic, swashbuckling response to life that many of us lose.

She represented an old self-connection I could tune into simply by thinking of her. So it was when I was going over some favorite quotes from years past, I imagined her responses

to them. They appeared in my head, spontaneous, strong—
Nothing's impossible. It just sometimes takes longer.
Ridiculous! *she retorts.*
If you go to bed with dogs, you get up with fleas.
Crock. Just get up.
If you're going through hell, keep going.
Silly.
No one cares how many storms you encountered—only if you brought in the ship.
Wrong! You may never bring in the ship, and it doesn't matter.
(You can see why I like her so much.) To my cry, "I have a horrible need of completion."
That is the most constipated thing I've ever heard.
That's attitude! And in regards to a personal sacred cow, which is my mantra, from Wordsworth:
Though none can bring back the hour
Of splendor in the grass, glory in the flower.
We will not grieve, rather find
Strength in what remains behind.
Absolutely.
"Only often no strength is left. Only remains," I say.
There's always strength. Life demands it! *she counters.*
Then there were two quotes concerning the failures we experience. First, Robert Louis Stevenson: "There is indeed an element in human destiny that not blindness itself can controvert. Whatever else we are intended to do, we are not intended to succeed; failure is the fate allotted....Our business is to continue to fail in good spirits."
Bless him, but leave it to Churchill to utter the ultimate inspiring comfort: "Success is moving from failure to failure with great enthusiasm."
Precisely.
Where had these jewels of coping therapy been all my

life? Those two homages to failures we experience popped out of books about the same time Sarah did.

Sarah. With all her theatrical hyperbole, she embodied self-acceptance and a fearless conscience. She shot from the hip boldly, without regard for reputation, in siding with the persecuted Jew in the Dreyfus Affair. After early acting flops and foreign tours (necessitated by an extravagant lifestyle, son and parasitic entourage), she dramatically manipulated comebacks. Phoenix-like, she regained critical and political audience approval. Never, whether acting on conscience or pleasure, would she pander to anyone for absolution.

A disdain for forgiveness accepts the price of things. The price of responsibility for the sum of one's actions is paid, head up, as a part of the offering one hands over at the end.

A courageous, defiant and gloriously self-accepting admission of failures, mistakes and indulgence, a refusal to be down. That was the essence of the actress's *esprit* with which I resonated.

The actress had her flaws. Among them, her reputedly poor sportsmanship when she lost in playing games is especially troubling to me. Certainly, one could cite the quality and quantity of her lovers as sign of a vanity and a certain insecurity.

Neither were you there, nor are you French, *she asserts.*

But to cite her quixotic taste in men or occasional tempestuous, careless treatment of others (usually reconciled by a contrite showering of gifts) or her breakfast bird shoot is to miss the point again.

Esprit is the French word for the whole package of personality, character, perspective and drive. *Esprit* has little to do with mistakes and weaknesses and everything to do with attitude and coping.

In Sarah Bernhardt's final days, the trooper that she was

rallied to act a final scene necessarily filmed in her home. Weak but courageous as always, she heavily rouged her face for a friend's visit and likely summoned her trademark laughter, so neither the friend nor she would be depressed.

Forecasting the Weather...

Loss and anxiety are generally linked together, unless we are talking weight loss. When the loss is the loss of the self, death anxiety projects forward and embodies many fears of unknowns ahead. Learning to cope better with all colors of big and small losses *now* will shorten the anxiety time and smooth every turn in the road when the actual physical process arrives.

As Woody Allen's character in *Anything Else* says, "I'd think of suicide, but I have so many problems, it wouldn't solve them all."

I am grateful Dr. Edwin Shneidman *has* thought of suicide. That he has done so in such therapeutically responsive and brilliant ways for its at-risk victims explains why he is held in highest peer regard. Thanks to his pioneer work in the field, *we can forecast how the weather will be when we are faced with a terminal diagnosis.* UCLA Professor Emeritus of Thanatology and founder of The American Association of Suicidology, Shneidman uses the metaphor of *rutters* to introduce *Voices of Death.*

Rutters, in the 16th and 17th centuries, were guidebooks or maps composed by those who had gone through dangerous routes and told all that was needed for a safe journey. Regarding how to "avoid the rough waters in the passage of our lives toward death, who of us would not want a personal rutter for dying written by a friendly pilot who had our best interests at heart?"[1]

Shneidman proceeds with the stories told by suicidal or nearly suicidal people, their coping patterns and particularly the relationship environments in their backgrounds. We can protest, "Hey! I'm not going to commit suicide, I just am going to have to die." But it is all part of the same package of rutters of what to avoid. Shneidman notes that disastrous relationships—such as fathers who reject you, adversarial mothers, non-affirming unloving relationships, and exploitative opposite sex partners—are deeply consequential losses.

Early identification and learning how to cope with these emotional wounds, if avoidance is impossible, develops the coping pattern that will surmount the obstacles of depression and fear in dying. Loss of the self is the biggest unavoidable loss of all. *His study of suicidal individuals and their patterns of coping can be applied to previewing how the rest of us will cope when faced with our supreme loss.*

Shneidman defines the following categories of death, among others. These should be understood in order to see where and how his insight fits those of us not overtly suicidal.

AN APPROPRIATE DEATH. Occurs when one is ready for it, at the right time and in the right way. This death is defined by Shneidman as appropriate to a person's time in life, his personal style, situation and mission in life as well as to the significant others in his life.[2] Some of the specific qualities it embodies, according to Dr. Avery Weisman, are "care, composure, communication, control, continuity and closure."[3] It's the ending you would choose for yourself if you could.

In *David Copperfield,* Barkus went out with the tide, for, as Mr. Peggotty tells David, along the coast one can't die "except when the tide's nigh out." With that sense of right timing, Barkus went out in sync, in tune with nature.

It is said that most people instinctively know when the moment is close at hand. Moreover, many complete a final goal because they are determined to do so before they die. Boston and Trezise [4] note that Pat Seed, who wrote *One Day at a Time*, was determined to raise one million pounds to buy a CAT scanner for Manchester's Christie's Hospital and held off dying until she did. There is also the famous example of timing and the strength of spirit over flesh which took place on July 4, 1826. Despite suffering, Thomas Jefferson wanted to live until the 50th anniversary of the signing of the Declaration of Independence. On that date he asked if it were the Fourth. When told that it was, he quietly died. Elsewhere, unbeknownst to each other, his old friend John Adams followed suit several hours later.

A SIGNIFICANT DEATH. For a cause or principle, as a sacrifice. In Mayan and other early athlete-warrior cultures, to be sacrificed in victory at the crowning, high point of life was an ideal. Profound to the Japanese culture, *hara kiri* and *seppuku* are ritual acts with meaning.

PARTIAL DEATH. Loss of one aspect of the self; a permanent, emotional emptiness. As Shneidman poignantly expresses it, "In a feelingless state the home fires are still burning but without the glow or warmth." Recognized by a number of us, this type of death-in-life is accompanied commonly by social withdrawal.

PSYCHOLOGICAL DEATH. A person's ceasing to be aware of his own existence. Although this is usually in tandem with clinical death, it is also the state associated with euthanasia and brain-death issues.

Shneidman further distinguishes between *intentioned, unintentioned and subintentioned deaths.* In the last the person has a covert, unconscious or subliminal part in hastening his own death. Archetypal is the obsessed Captain Ahab in *Moby Dick*. Shneidman's significant insight is that subintentioned, partial and intentioned deaths can almost always be attributed to some kind of loss. These include losses of a significant other (someone emotionally irreplaceable, such as a child), acceptance (i.e., rejection), self-esteem, health (a limb, eyesight, etc.), a job, finances, property, creative productivity or a stage in life. Even loss of a competition, a longed-for goal, familiar surroundings or other nurturing or protective security blankets is shattering for some.

When a loss occurs or is imminent, it is a person's innate coping ability that determines the outcome. With this single psychological fact as yardstick, it can be reasonably predicted how a person will handle stressful confrontation with the ultimate loss—the loss of self.

He further contends that *a person will bring to his or her terminal period the same coping mechanism used in previous periods of "threat, stress, failure, challenge, shock and loss...the course of an individual's life while he or she is dying over time, say of cancer, duplicates or mirrors or parallels the course of the life during its 'dark periods'; that is, one dies as one has lived in the terrible moments of one's life."*[5]

Shneidman and others have seen their perspective, that one's dying behavior is determined by previous, individualized coping patterns, as being at variance with Elisabeth Kubler-Ross's five stages—denial, anger, bargaining, depression and acceptance; these five are not necessarily consecutive and often overlap. It is true that frequently all or almost all five reactions are present, and it becomes a matter of degree and emphasis to identify them. However, in my experience, I found a few total anomalies whose resilience and attitudes defied stage-tagging. Instead, they followed a singular, healthy and rapid path to an acceptance of reality.

A close friend of mine was diagnosed with multiple myeloma, an incurable cancer of the bone marrow. She cried and spent many dark days not in denial or anger or bargaining, but rather went right to acceptance. The depression she felt came in great part from shock since she was then under 60 and incredibly fit and athletic. Also, initial depression appears to be the outward manifestation of death anxiety which embodies all the fears I researched. Such apprehension would have been understandably more intense in her case because of the abrupt, untimely nature of the news. Yet, she was determined to rally and gain a footing quickly.

Amazing me, she never felt sorry for herself or complained. She told me that her struggle with fear in the dark moments had but one objective: inner peace to get her through. She believed there was a lesson to learn which would move her ahead on her spiritual path, as much as she hated the lesson. Of course she wanted remission and was the doctors' prizefighter right through chemotherapy and stem-cell transplant. But her sight was, and remains, always on sustaining inner peace, no matter what the days might bring.

One great reason to toss out the concept of stages is the concern that *any* psychological pigeonholing method of assessment by professionals dehumanizes and undermines, albeit unintentionally, the distinctive attributes of each case. Rising above dissension, all these educators are on the same wavelength regarding the positive therapy of coping skills.

Some losses may produce heavy, reactive anger, but generally the anger masks fear underneath. Fear always projects forward, so we miss the peace of the present moment.

Coping skills can be taught and behavior patterns changed or modified, but it is tough. As Shneidman points out, individuals who are dying are rarely, if ever, "radically" inconsistent with themselves. They are stuck with their own backlogged arsenal of coping behaviors.[6] In "radically," there is hope and wiggle room, though! As is always the case, change takes determination and practice.

Some stumble into what works for them. About 16 years ago, before her illness, my friend felt dissatisfied and not truly happy. With a strong, supportive marriage, creative work and financial security, she was aware there was no real reason to feel in such limbo and began looking for a code to break it. She discovered, trusted and began practicing *A Course in Miracles*.

Two years after contracting multiple myeloma and reducing the cancer cells from 49% to a controllable area of less than 5%, my super-athletic, 61-year-old friend called me with disbelief and a few initial tears to say that a deep breast lump had appeared which ultrasound had confirmed. Breast cancer has no relationship to multiple myeloma!

This time, though, after only a few hours of numbness from shock, she realized that what she really was fearing was fear. In her case, she dreaded the roller-coaster emotional ride with fear just before every blood test and biopsy. "First peace, then apprehension creeps in, accelerates, whew!—terror fades. Peace again. I can't jump from track to track like this," she said, "and I choose peace."

Through meditation, a good Buddhist masters this discipline of holding to center no matter the weather. Focus is unwavering during the last hours of life. What an incomparable way to go that is, if you can!

I learned to cope well with past mistakes and failings by reminding myself that I had done the best I could at that moment in time. The most important rebirth in my coping pattern came spontaneously, perhaps as an instinctive survival mechanism, after a period of depression. I realized that, without any conscious effort, I had begun seeing the glass half full instead of empty after both big and small losses.

With the imminent loss of self, there are so many unknowns *ahead*. The anxiety experienced is a combination of fears, from fear of choking to death to fear of hell. It may come in waves; the first, when a life-threatening diagnosis is made; then again, waiting for the results of every test and bloodwork report; and finally, if and when no more can be done. Fear may come as the cold clammies or stomach dances at 2 A.M. because it is such a selfish beast. To deny those visceral moments of fear is to deny one's humanity. Only when there is little or no time to think are we spared the anxiety.

Violent or catastrophic trauma and instances such as instinctively diving in to save a drowning child seem to bypass initial confrontation with fear. Dr. Sherwin Nuland relates the eyewitness account of the serene face of a young girl brutally stabbed to death and how her mother felt "almost supernal warmth and the sense of being surrounded by a thick insulating aura." Otherwise, she believed she would have had a heart attack and died beside her daughter.

His opinion of this phenomenon? "Endorphin elevation appears to be an innate physiological mechanism to protect mammals and perhaps other animals against the emotional and physical dangers of terror and pain. It is a survival device, and because it has evolutionary value, it probably appeared during the savage period of our prehistory when life-threatening events occurred with frequency....The primitive pre-human whose heart and circulatory system did not succumb to sheer terror at the moment of the attack was the one who survived to have offspring whose responsiveness was much like his own."[7] Nuland surmises many lives have been saved by the absence of panic in sudden, perilous situations.

Moments of floating apprehension are unavoidable during a natural terminal illness. The length of time the fear feelings remain—that is something else. That is the work in coping skills we have to do. I, for one, want to be holding some trump cards to expedite the stay of those anxious feelings.

...and Dressing for It.

How many self-help books drone on with the message that it is not the cards you are dealt that matters, it is how you *choose* to react to them? Most often, we must get up close and personal as I did in my friend's circumstances to grasp that *choice* is a huge word in coping language.

With this insight in tow, what reactions should we avoid in seeking a better coping pattern for future losses? In answer,

Shneidman gives the characteristics of the suicidal person. They are in total preoccupation with the loss or trauma, severely constricting logic and perception, and inability to see options. Other elements he notes are a self-destructive, irregular pattern of living, failure, rejection and feeling cornered.[8] The trigger common to all ages of suicides is the loss of a close relationship, whether romantic, parental or other.

Particularly in light of the alarming rate of teenage suicide in recent decades, it warrants mention that the family unit can play a critical role in broadening the vision of options and strategic choices for any member who has sustained a loss. Recognizing these triggers and creatively addressing coping patterns, while we ourselves are young or while our children are, can impact society for generations to come and could not be more relevant to the subject of coping with the fears of dying later in life.

Smyth and Pennebaker report that writing personal and narrative accounts of very stressful events and confrontations improves mental and physical health.[9] Doing this simplifies, orders and gives structure to the past or current event. I see no reason why this would not be quite effective for those in the dying stage. Hospice guidelines encourage creating oral histories. A written assessment of one's profound emotions and thoughts about a terminal diagnosis and fears about dying would impose order and clear vision on what is usually a time of mental chaos.

The authors suggest writing for 30 minutes a day for 3-5 days. The more that causal and insightful words are used, usually in increasing number over the period, the more dramatic improvement resulted. One study showed coping improvement even among those who chose a stressful event to describe other than the chronic-pain condition they had.

Weisman singles out one key ingredient for optimum coping. *Strong morale,* achieved by whatever strategy or combination of strategies, should be the goal to develop and maintain. Morale is born in the conviction that we can free ourselves from past obstructions and then apply our liberation well. To master this ability we have no choice, he says, but to grasp willingly the consequences without deceiving ourselves about them or being in denial of them. Weisman notes that anger shows a lack of strategic responses. Anger is the most destructive, problem-causing reaction and is the hardest to deal with for the health care professionals, the patient-client and the support family alike.

A favored and most frequently *reported* strategy, he states, is to seek out information and guidance. Good copers also confront the problems; review and study alternatives and consequences; keep lines of communication, emotional expression and options open as well as stay flexible for correcting and moving between various strategies. Composure and a tolerance of distress are characteristic of good copers. They consider what is practical and feasible, cultivate confidence, set goals, track results and use collaboration.[10]

A favorite example of strong morale in terminal circumstances is Ulysses S. Grant. In a career marked with depression, business failures and heavy drinking, Grant was a decisive Civil War hero and an unremarkable president surrounded by corruption. All these characteristics can be used in apposition to his name.

What money he, with his family, retained after he left office was swindled from him by a friend. Money he subsequently borrowed from Vanderbilt was swindled from him. Again. Grant insisted on paying off the debt to Vanderbilt with what real estate he had. Although he contracted inoperable cancer, he doggedly followed Mark Twain's advice to write his memoirs. He pushed himself to the limit to do so for his family, although he died, penniless, four days after finishing them. His widow later received almost half a million dollars in book royalties.

Grant is an example of a life of commitment, failings, pain and perseverance and of a death with dignity and control. Take away the details and Grant's heroic moments of fame, and the hero remains and the story of many common people who would say "I could do no other," who called it simply doing what they had to.

Morale is the backbone of it all. Raising and maintaining it is the grand strategy and goal. Weisman points out that vulnerability is the antithesis of morale, and the key components of vulnerability are helplessness and hopelessness.

To this point, I append the place of humor. As long as it is not a mask for denial, a sense of humor can boost morale and be both the greatest compliment and complement to successful coping.

Morale and its component of humor, as antidote to vulnerability, bring to mind the two last utterances attributed to Oscar Wilde. Destitute but sipping champagne he sighed, "I am dying as I have lived, beyond my means." And, looking about the bedroom, "This wallpaper is killing me; one of us has got to go." Now that's morale!

Then there is fun, intellectual Jim Tucker, an elder but far from terminal friend. When the time comes, however, instead of an Obituary he threatens to write his personal Bitchuary, with enlightenment received crouched under his bonsai tree.

Humor.[11] Kastenbaum wrote, "To laugh at what makes us anxious is a form of mastery" through the employment of which we are able to transcend the fear. He notes that is why jokes told by older people who have come to terms with mortality tend to be more easy-going and good-natured than the fear-ridden, tense stories about death told by adolescents which mostly typify the "sick joke" category.[12]

When the opposing force of death arrives, the will can choose not to cringe but to remain standing in its presence.

A brush with death garnered a hospitalized Kastenbaum a profound learning rehearsal—he felt the presence of Big Mind, by whatever name. In *On Our Way*, I found his perception of unity with both the first human to die and the last yet to come a personal high point in my own journey.[13]

Another spiritual yet separate coping dimension triggered in life-threatening crises and during the physical process of dying needs highlighting. Having a religious anchor is likely to be a major coping component for a majority of Americans.

Why? Look at the polls. Bear in mind that, along with other findings and insights being presented and with the exception of the one turnaround attitude during the past 50 years already noted, the trends and statistics have been steady well over three decades. They are likely to continue thus for a number of years to come.

Do you believe in God or a universal spirit?

Year	"Yes" respondents
1994	96%
1978	94%
1953-54	99%
1947	94%

December 1994, Gallup Organization poll[14]

NOTE: The question extends beyond the monotheistic religions of Christianity, Islam, Judaism and Sikhism to a broad range of supernatural concepts.

This same poll reports that 93% believe in Heaven and, I love this one, 69% believe there is a good or excellent chance that they personally will go to Heaven. (Any mention of Heaven always reminds me of retired Episcopalian Bishop John Shelby Spong's comment[15] that 2000 years ago, ascending to Heaven's location upstairs in the clouds made sense at the time, but today we know that we would go into orbit instead.)

A USA Today-CNN-Gallup Poll in December 1999 reported 79% of Americans believe God will decide who goes to Heaven or Hell, and, a favorite statistic of mine from this poll, 44% believe good atheists will enter Heaven. Only 44% do?[16] Finally, a 1999 Poll by the *Survey Research Center at the University of California at Berkeley* reported that 86% of American Protestants believe in an afterlife, 83% of American Roman Catholics do and 74% of American Jews do.

Once again, though, because there are so many variables, such as other polls showing well over 50% believe in Hell, no clear numbers can be given for a link between lowered death anxiety and a belief in an afterlife. That the poll shows 69% are reasonably certain they will go to Heaven allows a leap of faith to the presumption that most Americans are fairly well squared away about their life after death. Personally, I think the issue is more complicated than this, with a lot more worms suddenly in the can when a life-threatening situation actually appears.

It is certain the spiritual component as a coping mechanism during a person's terminal process cannot be underestimated. Inclusive of but not dependent on this, the mainstream consensus is, as Robert Kavanaugh phrased it, that a life which has been spent in total commitment to anything or anyone outside of oneself—be it God, world hunger or science—is the broad key to good coping and inner peace during the final stage.

Two men who spent their careers assessing the coping responses of others are worthy examples here for what they themselves were called on to cope with in their own ultimate loss. Both Sigmund Freud and Carl Jung made sturdy confrontations with death. The reasons for the fortitude of each, and particularly for Freud's stoic courage, are significant reflections of Kavanaugh's and Robert Lifton's insights.

Nowhere was the contrast between the views of Freud and Jung more evident than in their opposing views of life after death. Becker points out that Lifton dubbed Jung's viewpoint as "mythic-hygienic"—good for the psyche.

Becker notes that although Freud mastered his fear of death throughout 16 horrible years with mouth cancer, he was most concerned with his *post-self* future in posterity's evaluation of his theories: Becker viewed that "Freud was toying ambivalently with yielding to transcendent powers, being very tempted in that direction."[17] He noted that Freud had trouble with yielding because it involved letting down his guard and exposing a lack of self-sufficiency.

Freud himself was a study in contradictions, exhibiting flickers of superstitions, attacks of death anxiety matched with a hero's resignation, fainting incidents, spiritualism and fears of helplessness and dependency. Yet he ostensibly remained a nonbeliever. *His inner sustaining spirit and courage at facing death are attributed to the ego strength derived from his reinforcing, maternal, childhood environment and his confident sense of self.* He endured his terminal period, replete with mosquito netting, flies and stench, armed with a heroic self-support system.

Death fascinated Jung. Yielding to a transcendent reality and the mystical dream plane of his unconscious was Jung's joy. He had a karmic sense of a pre-ordained destiny and could imagine being reborn again if he had not completed the task which God had assigned to him. His last days were dream-filled and serene.

Along with Jung particularly, Charles Darwin is another poster child for Kavanaugh's affirmation of a life lived in strong commitment and identity outside of oneself. Darwin would become physically ill whenever he went through periods of working on his evolutionary theories. He disliked the cruelty of nature he found in "the survival of the fittest" and disliked that his discoveries were contrary to the traditional Creator's immutable strokes.[18] Darwin even delayed publication of *On* the *Origin of Species* for 25 years, until 1859, for fear of the impact of its ideas: instead of being created by God, each thing evolves through mutation—survival of the strongest. He even experienced vomiting and dizziness before publication. These stress-induced illnesses appeared psychosomatic in their origin. After his final heart attack resulting from the chronic level of stress, he gave these last words to his family, "I am not in the least afraid to die."

Why was Darwin able to feel such serenity finally in the end, when all had been said and done? In answer to this one question every aspect of my research has been directed.

---

[1] Shneidman, Edwin. *Voices of Death*, New York: Harper & Row, 1980, p. 2.

[2] Ibid. *Deaths of Man*. New York: Quadrangle/The New York Times Book Co., 1973, and *Definition of Suicide*. New York: Wiley, 1985.

[3] Weisman, Avery D., M.D. *The Coping Capacity: On the Nature of Being Mortal*. New York: Human Sciences Press, 1984.

[4] Boston, Sarah, and Rachel Trezise. *Merely Mortal: Coping with Dying, Death and Bereavement*. London: Methuen, in association with Channel Four Television Co., Ltd., 1987.

[5] Shneidman. *Voices of Death*, p. 112.

[6] —. *Definition of Suicide*. New York: Wiley, 1985.

[7] Nuland, Sherwin. *How We Die*. New York: Knopf, 1994, p. 133.

[8] Shneidman. *Voices of Death*.

[9] Smyth, Joshua M., and James W. Pennebaker. "Sharing One's Story: Translating Emotional Experiences into Words as a Coping Tool." *Coping: The Psychology of What Works*. C. R. Snyder, ed. New York & Oxford: Oxford University Press, 1999, pp. 70-89.

[10] Weisman. Op. cit.

[11] It bears noting, with sadness, that humor is not an established characteristic of any religion except Zen Buddhism, an example of which begins Part III.

[12] Kastenbaum, Robert J., Ph.D., and Beatrice Kastenbaum, eds. *Encyclopedia of Death*. Phoenix: Oryx Press, 1989.

[13] Kastenbaum, Robert J., Ph.D. *On Our Way: The Final Passage Through Life and Death*. Berkeley & Los Angeles: University of California Press, 2004.

14 Gallup Organization. Poll, December 1994. Quoted in George Bishop. "What Americans Really Believe." *Free Inquiry*. Amherst. Summer (1999): 38-42.
15 Spong, John Shelby. Lecture. Westar Institute Millennium Symposium. Santa Rosa, CA. February 2000. A popular and highly respected author and speaker, the retired Episcopalian Bishop of New Jersey believes demythologizing Jesus is necessary if Christianity is to survive. In books and presentations he passionately calls Jesus his Lord, placing his main personal focus, search and faith on what it was in and about this man that caused people to express and feel such wondrous things about him.
16 USA Today-CNN-Gallup. Poll, December 1999. As cited in *Religion Today*, 29 December 1999.
17 Becker, Ernest. *The Denial of Death*. New York: Free Press, 1973, p. 106.
18 Panati, Charles. *Panati's Extraordinary Endings of Practically Everything and Everyone*. New York: Harper & Row, 1989.

CHAPTER 8

THE NEEDS OF THE DYING

> Q. *When your time comes, how would you wish to die?*
>
> *With the exception of the comical reply, "When I am 92 and at the hands of a jealous lover," most people would respond:*
>
> A. *At home, unexpectedly, in my own bed, when I am asleep, and when I am very old—but with my full mental and physical capabilities.*[1]

Three-fourths of Americans die of cancer, cardiovascular disease, AIDS, diabetes or liver, kidney and lung diseases and in institutional settings. One in four have hospice care. The fact, then, is that most Americans will not die as they would like—at home, a fact which can be a cause for anxiety in itself.

I found a unanimous consensus in my research. The two greatest fears in anticipation of one's terminal days are the fear of pain and the fear of dependency. Indeed, fear of dependency was the immediate response to my question of fears given by the hospice movement's founder Dame Cecily Saunders when I met with her at St. Christopher's Hospice in London.

By comparison, the Leming Death Fear Scale yielded low scores for fears related to the afterlife and the fate of the body. Specifically, 65% of more than 1,000 individuals surveyed had a high score regarding pain and dependency, while only 15% experienced that same anxiety level for matters such as eternal judgment, being buried, bodily decomposition, and so forth. "Thus it is the process of dying, not the event of death, that causes the most concern." ² This result leads to a key reminder: *It is dying only that we fear. We do not really fear death at all since we do not know it.*

Views and polls regarding primary death fears recall Ted Rosenthal's belief that people's fear of death is fear of an incomplete life. His was a more philosophical response to fear as the anxiety of regret, or even despair, in judging one's impending loss of self against the whole preceding life's course. Anxiety is apprehension of non-specified fears. The more classical definition of fear is a forward-projecting response to a specific danger or threat to one's well-being. The fears that rated highest in Leming's poll, those within the impending time frame of the process of physically dying, were more in line with the classical meaning of fear as a response to a specific imminent danger or threat.

Probably I, too, would identify the sensation of being unable to breathe as my primary fear and would identify the feeling of having wasted a lot of time and abilities as my primary anxiety, regret, despair. One is a blip; the other covers the whole screen.

How many operational levels death anxiety has within the psyche! Using fear and anxiety indistinguishably can overlook nuances that separate them. As far as repression versus intensity goes, I agree with and repeat the opinion that quite possibly the true names and scale of these fears for an individual may be only accurately measured when a life-threatening situation or diagnosis actually walks in the door.

Raymond Carey found more fear about pain in the dying process than about possible consequences after death and found an equally prominent fear to be the loss of one's loved ones and how they would cope afterwards. However, the number one concern in Carey's study was the fear of being a burden on others.[3]

Regarding the needs of the dying, a National Hospice

Demonstration Study centered around the following questions and responses. Kastenbaum and his colleague-superwife Beatrice were part of that research and training team, and she actually suggested these questions. Responses are in order from most to least frequently given.

A. Describe the last three days of your life and how you would like them to be.
1. I want certain people to be here with me.
2. I want to be physically able to do things.
3. I want to feel at peace.
4. I want to be free from pain.
5. I want the last three days of my life to be like any other.

Only one in twenty, reports Kastenbaum, cared about "completing a task" or being "mentally alert." Even fewer hoped to "accept death" (philosophically), and fewer still "wanted to know when death is imminent."

What is important, Kastenbaum notes, is that what most people wanted is no different from what hospice care aims for, in both its facility and in-home palliative practices—"the comfort of familiar faces and the ability to do a little for themselves and have a sense of peaceful routine." The support team should learn to respond to what really matters to each individual patient. Secret fears, such as of specific bodily distress, a family history of sudden death and bad theology based on reward, punishment and guilt can be critical information.

B. What will be your greatest sources of strength and support during these last days?
1. Supportive family and friends.
2. Religion.
3. Being needed.
4. Confidence in self.
5. Satisfied with the help received.[4]

Again, these are hospice goals. Meeting these needs goes a long way toward assuaging those fears perceived in the terminal physical process.

Another hospice goal is to make it possible for the patient to remain in the home with loved ones, if it is so desired. One glitch in obtaining hospice admission to in-home care is that there must be a primary caregiver, usually a spouse or family member, living with the patient for this period. Although a volunteer usually relieves the caregiver for some free time weekly, a significant other is required to reside with the patient to qualify for at-home care. Undaunted, I have a nest egg reserved just for that rainy day should I be facing dying without immediate family close by.

Several friends and I have already planned to be there for each other, with toasts not hankies. Although we haven't gotten around to assigning who gets the margarita shift and who searches the Web for jokes, the logistic truth is we all live in different cities. Besides, I would prefer their visits to vigils. There is a limit to how long I can cheerfully endure X's yappy dog in my tiny abode and Y's phone fetish. (And it is a sure bet my tolerance isn't going to be any better then. Hearing is the last sense to go.) Consequently, I have the following ad put away in a drawer.

WANTED

Live-in female caregiver to qualify privacy-loving elderly woman for home hospice admission. Sense of humor and open mind imperative. Experience with dying, not experience dying, required. Light housekeeping, driving. Nice room and garden setting.

Certain anticipatory steps predictably can ease a person's period of adjustment to the final stage. Carey's study revealed the most important factors are "the level of discomfort, previous close contact and talking openly with a dying person, religious orientation, a feeling of great interest and concern on the part of one's nearest of kin and local clergyman, and amount of education."[5]

Related to religion in the broad sense, it was important to have integrated their beliefs into their lifestyles and practiced them. In the narrow sense, Christians appeared to be better emotionally adjusted than non-Christians. "Education was also positively related to emotional adjustment, possibly because both are related to financial security," Carey writes in *Death: The Final Stage of Growth.*

Further checkpoints of comfort are ego strength at the onset of the terminal illness, the sense of having lived a full life, an honest and supportive relationship with one's doctor and loved ones. This includes a mutual giving of permission to let go. (I heard this confirmed as special and needed by numerous families following the death of their member.)

More checkpoints of comfort are having finances squared away, maintaining control and being respected.[6] A number of thanatologists, including Carey, would add a sustained hope of a joyful afterlife.

Regarding specific fears and general anxiety about the terminal period held by those in good health, though, there is one consensus that allays them. I cannot emphasize enough that the medical consensus among doctors is that most people are ready to die when the time comes. They feel both physically and psychologically functioned out after a prolonged period of cancer, AIDS or disorders of a bodily system that has finally worn out. The complex reactions of a young person or the distress of someone who regrets (or worse, has guilt) that he or she "didn't make the most" of a life time give way to readiness.

The acceptance that the quality of life has gone can be comforting rather than depressing. It also is a great consolation to the bereaved, who many times have told me so. Going one step further to accept the foreknowledge that we will feel functioned out this way and that excellent, often total pain control and lucidity are realistic expectations are potent antidotes to heightened death anxiety in our younger and middle years.

To my knowledge, this common-sense truth is never highlighted. But from my experience with those who are dying and those who are left, its coping value cannot be overestimated.

With this one realization keeping them company, here are the big four requisites to getting through, moment to moment, the culminating weeks and hours. They embrace both the patient and all the personal and professional supporters who contribute to the dignity and meaning of this time.

The Main Four

Schulz and Schlarb report that more than 80% of deaths in the United States have at the *least* two weeks' warning, and 50% live with the knowledge at the *least* three months.[7] The rights of the patient, those the vast majority of us would wish for ourselves during this time span, are as follows.

1. To mean something to someone
The therapeutic need of a close, intimate connection with another, a relationship between two, is an axiom throughout the published annals of all death education, including the teachings of every major world religion. As Dr. Oostvogel expressed it, "Most important of all for the patient is to have somebody around who really cares and is willing to listen."[8]

Dr. Kubler-Ross urged hospital chaplains to sleep during the day and work at night when most people die and need a relationship to receive the fear, pain and loneliness.[9] How and when the patient relates to his or her doctor is critical.

Dr. Peter Selwyn attends terminal AIDs patients in their final stage. He never came to terms with the sudden death of his father when he was eighteen months old. He finally confronted and grieved this primal loss.

Afterwards, he found it easier to be with his patients in their pain, "to support them without feeling the blind compulsion to rescue them from something from which there was no rescue, and to stay with them as they approached death without feeling that I had somehow betrayed their trust. I have learned that the greatest gift that I can give patients is to allow the awareness of my own pain and loss to deepen my solidarity with them as they face their illness and death. I am now convinced that it is the physician's fear of death, and his or her own unexpressed grief, that are the biggest impediments to true empathy, and result instead in pity, despair, revulsion, and the kind of numbing detachment that finds refuge in technological interventions and narrow medicalization."[10]

Dr. Selwyn's patients are fortunate.

Once, while a friend ran out to the grocery, I sat at his mother's bedside on what turned out to be the day before she died. She was in his home, and between his family, other members flying in frequently and her young grandchildren popping into her room even more frequently with holsters and dripping Disney towels, she was completely encircled with love. Referring to her dying and these last days, she made a comment to me I will never forget. "I couldn't go through this without them."

Those seven words say more than all of mine about the importance of others during this time. Or these seven last words of Henry James: "Stay with me, Alice, stay with me."[11]

Surely, nowhere was the indomitable spirit of man in the face of death more tested than in a Nazi death camp. Viktor Frankl persevered through the days by having mental conversations with his wife, holding her image always before him, not knowing if she were dead or alive. "There was no need for me to know; nothing could touch the strength of my love, my thoughts, and the image of my beloved....Love is as strong as death."[12] For Frankl, home was wherever his wife was. The significance of such a relationship during a terminal period also has meaning for those who do not die in the home. Home can well be wherever the beloved is.

There is another relationship represented by good theology. For believers, communion with a Spiritual Power can be the dying person's most therapeutic, intimate and deepest two-party connection. If one dies alone, it can be "everything."

Apart from the dying one's own inner communion, the bedside role of an intercessor with a higher being or cosmic unity historically has been critical to all major religions since primitive man. It is a role taught by the holy books of instruction to the Egyptian, Hindu, Buddhist and Christian.

To both the Hindu and Buddhist, one's state of mind at death determines one's state after death. The other person plays a vital role in helping the dying maintain self-control and focus positively within his or her mind. To be without fear and thinking right almost assures a fine comeback or the ultimate bliss of not coming back!

Muslim family and friends sit at the deathbed reciting the Qur'an. There are tremendous variations, as well as unresolved conflicts, in dying beliefs and practices within Islam, which is derived from many sources including and beyond the Qur'an. Basic is the belief in a single God, Allah, and a second eternal existence for the soul after death. Ira Lapidus states, "Death is the ultimate test of a Muslim's capacity to accept God's decree with fortitude and trust."

This attitude, Lapidus points out, on one hand can be fatalistic but, on the other, provides a stoic wisdom, strength and consolation in the trials. "Between death and the resurrection there is an intermediary phase, the life of the grave. [Some but not all believe] Death and the life of the grave are a fearsome experience," as is the suffering when the soul and body are separated. Varying degrees of terror and judgment abound among the faith's different shadings and opinions. There is communication between the dead and the living through dreams and visions as well as the dead acting as intercessors to God.[13]

A major force in the world, the Muslim faith represents a fast-growing percentage of the U.S. population. If we are to survive well together, it behooves the community, particularly the medical one, to appreciate and respect the religious context and inner focus surrounding the dying Muslim patient.

In the medieval Anglican bestseller *The Rule and Exercises of Holy Dying* (1651), its section "The Manner of Visitation" dictates that if the person is too infirm to make his own supplications, then they are to be "supplied by the acts of the minister and standers-by, who are in such cases to speak more to God *for* him" than to talk to him. The vast majority of the U.S. is faith-based. Whether in formal rituals or loose, spiritual communication, throughout history these closing relationship scenes have enacted more than religious traditions. *They are human covenants.*

The dying person may hear and feel even after others think he or she no longer can. In the end, above all, are touch and a caring voice. Hearing is generally the last sense we lose. From the patient's perspective, a feeling of love and significance to another never ends.

Given the importance of supportive relationships during the final days, it is amazing that a problem can be overlooked for couples and single people who relocate in late life or retirement. This alert comes from my experience with families in a retirement bedroom community and an urban city. Couples or singles who move to sunny locales to walk on the beach may be thoughtlessly leaving a support system of long-term friendships and especially that of having grown children nearby.

Take an elderly couple who move to a retirement climate where they live contentedly with each other's company and some travel. The man dies, leaving an 85-year-old nearly blind widow, at a loss to even see, much less negotiate the bus and senior retirement center. Their children have flown out occasionally but always must return to their jobs in the city in which they all once lived.

I stress this scenario because where children and grandchildren live in proximity, the beneficial difference to everyone can be tremendous. As for those without children, friends through thick and thin are family. I am not smugly preaching—I relocated away from a strong support system before my death education began.

All alone. Abandonment is a primal fear. Dying can be more fearful if experienced alone, yet that is always a possibility. I found a history lesson which is translatable to those today who may be alone, for whatever reason, in an institution or at home in the last hour or so as the body and consciousness close down.

Going back to the second half of the 15th century, large-edition woodcuts could be produced in large, inexpensive series. Because of frequent epidemics and the scarcity of priests given the number of victims, many faced dying alone. What did they do? Arthur Imhof tells us, "They *learned* to die....Even if they could not read, they could look at woodcuts. In the view of that time, a soul's fate was often decided during the last hour on earth."

For them the education took the form of a small brochure of eleven woodcuts, five illustrating the temptations of faith, despair, pride and arrogance, impatience and worldly materialism. The second five illustrated the heavenly brigade hastening to his support: angels, saints and the Trinity. With the latter's help in the battle for the soul, he would die. The eleventh portrayed the happy ending of an angel's welcoming reception of the soul, now a small, naked child being introduced into God's radiance. "Dying, the *right* way of dying, could be learned....One knew what the last hour held in store, and one had only to copy Everyman on the woodcuts to be assured eternal bliss."[14]

Imhof proposes that we must find an *ars moriendi*, an art of dying right, that is also accessible to *everyone* today, *faith-based or not*, one that is rooted in the reality of current ideologies and the possibility of dying alone. Pointing out that both life expectancy and expectancy of *good* years have well more than doubled, he suggests that the execution of an actual life plan of fulfilling stages will result in dying right. This recalls the goal of D-Day and life review exercises. It also reflects the consensus that *a life planned by commitments to something greater than itself* will bring all the peace one needs to transcend anxiety at life's conclusion.

In their last hours our forebears' learnéd practice with the visual imagery of the woodcut series is similar to the discipline exercised in Eastern cultures. For a peaceful transition and future, the dying person lets go of any negative emotion of anger, attachment or fear to focus intently on the positive emotions of compassion and love and images of the divine as personally understood or beauty anticipated and hope projected for the awaiting future.

Just as the woodcuts, these images become emotionally charged relationships. They are rutters we will be able to turn to and rely on.

However, there is a Buddhist alert to heed—that these must not represent clinging attachments in this life, such as to those who may be around your bed. A more creative and important visualization to have ready I cannot imagine.

2. To be pain-free

We have a right to claim whatever pain-free experience is

available. As one doctor assured, you can be guaranteed no pain, even if anesthesia drugs are utilized in a pinch.

Pain is not a synonym for dying, but chronic pain is the symptom most feared. The facts: Even in patients with widespread cancer, one in three experiences little or no pain. Now, even for the others, with narcotics often in combination with common non-steroid, anti-inflammatory drugs, dying with adequate pain relief is a realistic expectation.

If the pain dissipates, morphine and other opioids can be discontinued by gradual reduction. There is, however, a current controversy, due to conflicting studies, over the addiction capability of some of these drugs. Heretofore, a 75% immediate reduction was thought possible without problems. The verdict is out on the degree of possible addictive residue for those who go into remission or recover. A good number believe as long as there is a true need of the drug, there will be little if any withdrawal problem if or when the pain no longer exists. The issue of addiction should not be a consideration during this time. In sum, the goal is that the pain feared in the past be exactly that—in the past.

Contributors to *Pain, Anxiety, and Grief* address the other real component of pain control, the psychological one. Goldberg points out that as depression can intensify pain, hypnosis can reduce or totally alleviate it for some. As an echo to Blacker's belief in the effective ability of a caring physician's calming words and presence to greatly lessen anxiety, Seeland states, "It is a fact that human contact provides better relief for anxiety than drugs do" and that physical suffering itself responds dramatically to therapy other than with drugs.[15] Here again, as an anxiety and analgesic prescription, a caring relationship ranks at top place.

Dr. Elizabeth Lee's book *In Your Own Time* systematically reviews the various common complaints and the wide choice of drugs available to relieve each. I choose not to list these medicines by name, since one's doctor is best qualified to prioritize them. However, here are the main assaults during this period and a few comments.

This is a book about fears of death, and is it not impossible to imagine someone in mortal fear of bed sores? Ditto nausea, constipation, vomiting, loss of bladder and bowel control, loss of appetite and mouth sores? All of these can be effectively combated. However, there can be varying layers of anxiety to these areas of discomfort. For example, Dr. Ira Byock writes of a constipated male patient in *Dying Well*. His impacted bowels were a source of anxiety and self-conscious embarrassment since nurses regularly would have to manually disimpact him. For such anxiety concerning exposure of bodily functions perceived as degrading, Dr. Byock has a strong message that deserves footlights. *People "are only made undignified if they are placed in situations that are demeaning."* [16] *He stresses that nurses and doctors see ministering to these end-of-life needs as extremely dignified and privileged work.*

I would suggest also that just as we minister to a baby's needs, the circle of life involves interdependent ministry to both coming and going. As we have done for those births and deaths before and after us in our children, parents and community, so they do for us in our times of need.

Depression and sleeplessness are likewise treatable with myriad therapeutic responses, which is commonplace knowledge. Two others also hold frightening prospects— difficulty in breathing and confusion. Choking with difficult breathing is my own personal dread. In actuality, Lee says, "Patients hardly ever choke to death and you need not fear this. The natural mechanism of the body allows you to fall into unconsciousness as your breathing deteriorates." [17]

She adds that recent studies have shown also that almost all sufferers of motor neuron disease die peacefully. She notes that there are many causes for breathlessness, such as heart failure, pleuron effusion or fibrosis of the lung, and different treatments to match each including several well-known pills to reduce the sensation as well as sitting upright, even inclined forward slightly. Important to know is that the irregular and labored breathing, and the noise of saliva in the throat you may have noticed in others' dying, is called Cheyne-Stokes breathing. It is hard only on the observer. Almost always, the patient has long since gone into a coma when this commences and so is not bothered or in distress.

Confusion is perhaps particularly frightening because it emphasizes dependence on others. However, Lee notes, most patients retain no fear when they are confused, and there is treatment for those who are upset. Late stage confusion is common and due to any number of causes, among them dehydration, an increasing level of urea in the bloodstream as kidneys fail, certain drugs which can be adjusted, infection and so on. Severe constipation and high levels of circulating calcium can also be culprits and are treatable.

There can be ebbs and flows with total clarity, Lee notes, and it is important to preview and explain these as much as possible to the patient. Long-term memory is stronger than recent memory, rational thought is not to be expected and patience will be a boon, Lee reminds.[18] Before then, the last days and even hours without pain and with clarity of mind and speech can and do occur. Supposedly, the exit lines of the actor Douglas Fairbanks were "Please open the window and let me hear the sea....I've never felt better." What a great closing camera shot and fade-out that image conjures up! His request leads directly to the next but *far* from least of the considerations caregivers can give the patient.

3. *To retain control of the process and its quality*
A huge component of the fear of losing control and

dependency can be resolved right now, if it has not been already, by filling out Advance Directives. These are a Living Will, Advance Directive to Physicians and Medical Power of Attorney, or however these are legally titled in respective states.

It is imperative to do this, and nothing justifies dawdling. Saying one hasn't made up one's mind exactly is no excuse. Make it up now. You can always alter them if your views do. *If you don't have a fear of death without them, you should have!* Our last days should be spent according to our wishes, not those of the State.

The dying person should have control of the experiences and have the reins to be heard, understood and able to leave the gifts of words he chooses. The situation in which the patient has authority should be as similar to life before illness as possible. It should be a take-charge time, creative, with all the variables of personality determining its course.

Trelease's study of Alaskan Indians in *Death: The Final Stage of Growth* relates a common practice among the dying. A person calls family and friends together so that he or she may pray for those about to be left. It appears, Trelease notes, that members of this ethnic group can intuit and seemingly regulate the time of death until the last cousin makes it across the tundra.[19]

4. To have respect

In the midst of tubes and bedpans, the feeling of respect the patient receives from personal and medical supporters is priceless. A senior staff member at London's St. Christopher's Hospice recalled a patient who requested no pain medication towards the end. Knowing the patient's prior easy adjustment to the medicine, the nurse had some rational trouble with the decision but respectfully abided by it.

Among those of Jewish faith, the bedside tradition of constant vigilance and community involvement provides the setting for the passing on of wisdom and ethical education to the next generation. This wonderful custom, a culminating rite of passage, affords the dying person not only ongoing dignity and value, but also peak fulfillment in bestowing on the next generation the unique insights learned from the sum of years.

Thus, a two-way listening relationship, having meaning for and the respect of others, the control of putting one's house in order, dying in comfort—these four say it all.

Dr. Byock has an acutely observant poet's eye for his terminal patients. One in particular, Mo, stood out for her meaningful internal integration of this final process. She conveyed a sense of her fluid identity moving on, a person growing "on out of life...into pure spirit," he writes. Privileged to have attended such patients in their final moments, he describes the transition which others, like myself, lacking his eloquence, may have witnessed as well.

"At the edge of the transcendent—in the midst of 'letting go'—a person who has completed the work of development does not disintegrate in dying. Rather she *dissolves* out of life, becoming increasingly ephemeral—less dense or corporeal—but no less integrated, in the passage from life. Personhood becomes gauzy and translucent. Having completed and released the various realms and spheres of his or her previous self, the person who is surrendering to the transcendent is little more than the process itself. 'Letting go' is all that is left." [20]

---

[1] Leming, Michael R., and George E. Dickinson. "The American Ways of Death." *The Unknown Country: Death in Australia, Britain and the USA.* Kathy Charmaz, Glennys Howarth and Allan Kellehear, eds. New York: St. Martin's Press, 1997, p. 175.

[2] Ibid.

[3] Carey, Raymond. "Living Until Death: A Program of Service and Research for the Terminally Ill." *Death: The Final Stage of Growth.* Dr. Elisabeth Kubler-Ross, ed. Englewood Cliffs, NJ: Prentice-Hall, 1975, pp. 75-86.

[4] Kastenbaum, Robert J., Ph.D. *Death, Society, and the Human Experience.* 8th Ed. Boston: Allyn and Bacon, 2003.

[5] Carey. Op. cit., p. 79.

[6] Ibid., pp. 75-84.

[7] Schulz, Richard, and Janet Schlarb. "Two Decades of Research on Dying: What Do We Know About the Patient?" *Omega: Journal of Death and Dying.* Robert J. Kastenbaum, Ph.D., ed. Farmingdale, NY: Baywood. 18.4 (1987-88): pp. 299-319.

[8] Oostvogel, F.J.G., Dr. "A Terminal Care Project in a Nursing Home in the Netherlands." *Death and Dying: A Quality of Life.* Patricia Pegg and Erno Metze, eds. Bath: Pitman, 1981, p. 71.

[9] Gill, Derek. *Quest: The Life of Elisabeth Kubler-Ross.* New York: Harper & Row, 1980.

[10] Selwyn, Peter A. "Before Their Time: A Clinician's Reflections on Death and AIDS." *Facing Death: Where Culture, Religion, and Medicine Meet.* Howard M. Spiro, Mary G. McCrea Curnen and Lee Palmer Wandel, eds. New Haven & London: Yale University Press, 1996, p. 35.

[11] O'Kill, Brian. *Exit Lines (and not-so-famous) Last Words.* Essex, England: Longman, 1986.

[12] Frankl, Viktor E. *Man's Search for Meaning.* New York: Touchstone Ed., 1984, p. 50.

[13] Lapidus, Ira M. "The Meaning of Death in Islam." *Facing Death.* Op. cit., pp. 148-159.

[14] Imhof, Arthur E. "An Ars Moriendi for Our Time: To Live a Fulfilled Life, to Die a Peaceful Death." *Facing Death.* Op. cit., pp. 116-18.

[15] Seeland, Irene Dr. "The Cancer Ward." *Pain, Anxiety, and Grief: Pharmacotherapeutic Care of the Dying Patient.* Ivan K. Goldberg, Austin H. Kutscher and Sidney Malitz, eds. New York: Columbia University, 1986, p. 163.

[16] Byock, Ira, Dr. *Dying Well: The Prospect for Growth at the End of Life.* New York: Riverhead, 1997, p. 95.

[17] Lee, Elizabeth, Dr. *In Your Own Time: A Guide for Patients and Their Carers Facing a Last Illness at Home.* New York: Oxford University Press, 2002, p. 191.

[18] Lee. Op. cit., pp. 157-205.

[19] Trelease, Murray L. "Dying Among Alaskan Indians." *Death: The Final Stage of Growth.* Op. cit., pp. 33-37.

[20] Byock. Op. cit., p. 238.

Je vais querir un grand peut-etre.
(I am going to seek a great perhaps.)
—legendary last words
of Francois Rabelais

PART III

WHAT THEN?

The fears of nothingness, judgment
and the unknown

A nobleman asked Master Hakuin, "What happens to the enlightened man at death? What happens to the unenlightened man?"

The master replied, "Why ask me?"

"Because you are a Zen master!"

"Yes," said Hakuin, "but not a dead one!"

—**Master Hakuin (1686-1769)**

Life is—or has—meaning and meaninglessness. I cherish the anxious hope that meaning will preponderate and win the battle.

—**Carl Jung**

Part III is about afterlife challenges and resolutions.

Chapter 9

The Cons of an Afterlife Belief

So there our climber is, about to fall off the cliff, holding on to a branch and hoping, if he is among the majority of Americans, that there is a God up there to save him. He lets go, and what happens? *Kerplat?* A welcome mat? Or a bed of coals?

Francis Bacon wrote, "Men fear death as children fear to go in the dark; and as that natural fear in children is increased with tales, so is the other." From the beginning, humankind has needed to create something there in the dark to quell our fears and fill the dark void of the unknown. Something friendly that won't let us die.

For two thousand years before Christianity took over the function in the West, the mystery rites at Eleusis held people's hopes of continuance after death. At this spot in Greece and elsewhere in cultures on all continents, death and rebirth ceremonies were enacted to give the initiate confidence in facing death by bringing him or her into the presence and protection of the gods of the underworld. But it has been the secrets of the Eleusinian Mysteries which have captured the imaginations of scholars and mystics alike. Such was their impact, Cicero observed in *De Legibus* that the Eleusinian Mysteries were Athens' highest contribution to the world. When you consider their competition, both in philosophical and democratic concepts, that's strong!

We know little of these transforming rites except that the focal agrarian cycle, the regeneration of a new crop, was the symbol for eternal life. The initial cleansing ritual of bodily bathing has everything in common with the purification ceremonies of baptism today and strict Islamic post-mortem preparation. The figurative aspect of this cleansing is not unlike the awakening brought about by the process of Twelve-Step programs. Certain other Eleusinian elements of mystic food, fasting and a passion play have their sacramental parallels in contemporary renewal rituals also.

Aries looks to death's historical place as a hallowed and purifying rite of passage. In French art of the Middle Ages, he notes the soul at the moment of death was symbolized by a naked, even sexless, child. The dying person exhaled the child from his mouth so that the soul departed in an image of a child's innocence and purity.[1] The soul survived death because of a cleansing renewal and rebirth.

Whether in pagan Greece, medieval Christian Europe or elsewhere in world cultures and chronology, transforming preparations for salvation have relied on a source beyond the Self for deliverance from anxieties either in this life or about the next one. The connection at Eleusis with archetypal mythic spirits in the other world has its more concrete reflection today in the reassuring connection of psychic mediums with the deceased. Humanity's yearnings for something wonderful in the dark have not changed. *But is that need the source of evil?*

Some cons
In *Escape from Evil* Ernest Becker makes a case for man's denial of his mortality—in his attempt for a heroic self-image through the attainment of the power of immortality—as being the reason for human evil.

Primitive man chose to create an economic surplus beyond his basic needs. Through religious, sacrificial offerings, his desire was to appease the controlling gods of nature. This innately ceremonial "cosmology of obligation and expiation" kept the bounty given to man in balance with man's repayment to the invisible, transcendent forces.

Defining the hero—since early history where the examples were of warrior and hunter—as the one who successfully defies death, Becker points out that those who showed supernatural abilities were responsible for the first class distinctions. Those who were deemed the darlings of the gods got obedience and respect and thereby dominated mere mortals. Thus, the case can be made for the origin of inequality, the subjugating domination and power of one individual over another, as traceable to man's innate thirst for immortality.

People or things that represented the power of immortality answered the people's need for a visible god, a Pharaoh, who favored their offerings and granted them prosperity. Becker called this the natural genius of primitive man: to provide himself with what he needed most—daily affirmation that he was living right in God's sight, and that his mundane, everyday work had cosmic value, and that it in fact enriched and improved God himself! Indeed, the utterance of the Pharaoh's name was followed in the same breath with "life, prosperity and health." The *self-proclaimed divination* of all such emperors *not only established their source of power, but also constituted moral consolidation.* So, in his opinion, began the evolution of tyranny.

Becker makes the observation that Christianity tried but failed to give salvation back to the individual. It did not eradicate economic inequality and subjugation. Therefore, he states, never since primitive society has the basic structure of domination and exploitation by the state changed. Wealth has been another symbol of immortality power. It is interpreted as money or gold to purchase goods or enduring monuments to leave behind as a testament to one's enduring image through the immortality of the tangible estate. Both gold, whether in terms of a pyramid or corporation, and power have been major goals in man's drive to deny death and overcome insignificance. Often, both have been attained at the blood expense of others.

The "shadow" in each psyche is a Jungian metaphor for one's awareness of his or her inferior or creature nature, in spite of the attempt to deny it. One way of freeing oneself of guilt or the knowledge of one's "shadow" is by projecting this negative image onto others or an outside entity. Both individually and collectively, this projection of imperfection defines the scapegoat's position historically. Becker gives the example of genocide efforts by the Nazis of the Jews and Poles.

Another argument tying the desire for immortality to the cause of human evil is what he calls the principle of immortality striving. He quotes Rank, "Every conflict over truth is in the last analysis just the same old struggle over...immortality." (An example easily understood is, "If your adversary wins the argument about truth, you die.") If your immortality-ideology system is found to be fallible, then your life is fallible. Even though beliefs changed from culture to culture, century to century, he maintains that this principle remained a constant.[2]

Whether or not you agree with Becker's overall thesis, certainly there is ground for agreement that, broadly viewed in sociological terms, man's fear of death and his hunger to survive it have played compelling roles in shaping history.

Misplaced reverence

There is a living entity whose sickness and death will matter far more than our own, for we are dependent on it for life itself. If it dies, it cannot be recreated. Yet, we remain homocentric in our relationship to the true ground of all being, the earth. In our vernacular "heaven" opposes "earth," and "sacred" is other-worldly. In *Sacred Gaia, Gaia's Gift* and *Making God Laugh*, Dr. Anne Primavesi, a systematic theologian at the University of London, reminds that ecological takes precedence over human history, and that without ecology there can be no economy, no sustainability of any species.

Religions and their institutional leaders have misplaced

dependency issues. Their cameras have held an anthropocentric view of life and the God who created that human life. Primavesi writes of the interdependent community of all life as embodied in the Gaia theory developed by James Lovelock. For her, the spirituality of Gaia, the planetary life-support system, encompasses God's relationship with all living creatures, including those before *homo sapiens* appeared. Our lives depend "on continuous tight bonding between all life and its physical and chemical environment—[Gaia theory shows] that the presence and strength of that bond depends ultimately on the gift of energy from sun to earth."[3]

All life on earth is sun-dependent. Primavesi turns to an observation on our sun-centered selves by Buddhist teacher Thich Nhât Hanh in *The Sun My Heart*. "We know that if our heart stops beating, the flow of our life will stop, and so we cherish our heart very much. Yet we do not often take the time to notice that there are other things, outside of our bodies, that are also essential for our survival. If [the sun] stops shining, the flow of our life will also stop, and so the sun is our second heart, our heart outside of our body. This immense 'heart' gives all life on earth the warmth necessary for existence."[4]

In *Making God Laugh*, Primavesi uses "more than human" instead of "non-human" in text references to other species. She points to the humbling ecological fact that the human epic is a small fraction of planetary time and design. She suggests the arrogant fundamentalist claim to speak on behalf of God's plan would make God laugh if that claim did not have such catastrophic consequences.

Christian ministers preach the Kingdom of God yet do not connect Jesus' words to the reality that is spread before us on Earth in its natural resources and supporting climate. The Gospel of Thomas well understood where and what the divine domain was: "Split a piece of wood, lift up a stone, ask the sky, birds and fish for they have known where I am all along," Jesus says. Yet the abuses and plunder of Gaia's gifts continue.

Is the momentum of mysterious new viruses in birds and beasts a growing warning signal? Humans steadfastly refuse to accept a secondary place in a geocentric spirituality focused on reverence and responsibility for this space and this moment. Misplaced, their reverence is instead for another space and future moments beyond Earth.

Further cons

Other arguments against the greedy thirst for immortality and what it has caused are manifold. The persuasive biological one against afterlife is obvious. Consciousness is a function of the brain. The brain organ dies. The other, less evident, perspective is definitely food for humanitarian thought.

Apart from Becker, other secular death educators express similar observations. Kavanaugh writes:

> Undue occupation with the whether of an afterlife has ruined untold numbers of lives with unnecessary fears. It has split families and impoverished tribes which put riches and even people into tombs. It has put too much magical power into the hands of religious leaders, often distracting them from godliness. It has deferred the social progress of mankind in dealing with poverty, ignorance, disease and war, deferring until another life the insistent needs and demands of today. About the only good I can see is that our over-preoccupation has been good for the economy....*I find by experience that men remain morally the same without belief in afterlife, and maybe nonbelievers work harder to make this world a moral and happier place because it is all they have.*[5]

Are nonbelievers sometimes even morally *better* without an afterlife belief? Always there have been religionists who walked a humanitarian path, not merely an individually based one. Yet, the question presents itself in looking, for example, at the caste system in India, whether a fixating vision of heaven, or an afterlife rewards system of justice, or concept of karma in this case, prevents attention and responsibility for realities in the here and now.

Hinduism, centered around reincarnation and the accumulation of karma, has come far in lip service, mainly rethinking class segregation and condemnation. However, the vestiges of a mentality persist that believes outcasts are born deserving of their meet in life and must take responsibility for it. This has given tacit approval to horrific economic conditions for massive numbers. As Gandhi said, "If untouchability [of nearly 40 million Hindus in India in 1968] lives, Hinduism perishes, and even India perishes; but if untouchability is eradicated from the Hindu heart, root and branch, then Hinduism has a definite message for the world."[6]

Examples of the manipulation of believers, as witnessed in the Crusades as well as in religious intolerance and fanaticism alive in countries today, also portray this dark side. Kastenbaum minces no words: "The promise of a happy ever after has itself contributed to some of the most vicious behavior ever seen on this planet....Most of the killers were people who believed in their respective religions and who believe in some form of survival after death."[7] On this topic, consensus and a complete airing of all points are impossible.

Here, briefly, are my favorite "con" arguments for why we need to reassess what our fears have created and how we have ignored and been deaf to the true messages of respective spiritual leaders. (The chameleon I am will appear in the next chapter).

First, Heaven is without geographical credibility. We want to be reborn into a magical kingdom, not grow up in this one by facing some facts. The world, or people's understanding of it, is not what it used to be. Until over 15 centuries after the times of Jesus, the earth was believed to be flat. The sky was a canopy over it, and going up just out of sight after death was imaginable. Today, we know we would be in orbit. Where exactly are we joining God? If God is a Being, then It has to have weight and take up space.

Second, if God is a feeling or concept like Love or Justice, which are certainly real, then the good news is there will be no judgment to fear, and, likewise, the bad news is there will be no reward. That leaves reincarnation a possibility, with final cosmic unity. Impotent to forgive and save, God then is a homeless traffic cop giving karmic directions to impulse patterns!

Third, there have been a lot of innocent animals and humans brutally sacrificed, a lot of blood mixed with wine for salvation and a lot of bodies dirtied during life which at death were made squeaky clean, all in preparatory initiation for an afterlife.

Evolving primitive societies and their religions went from women being chattel and gods sacrificing their sons to a flat earth and an eternal romp in the clouds when they died. All these doctrines have evolved but the last.

The worst disconnect which remains is the principle of the Atonement. What god would want his son tortured on a cross for *any* reason? Who could ever trust or want such a barbaric god?

Today, bloodbaths continue to take their toll from the world. Competing, monotheistic, afterlife systems and their prophets vie. In Western culture, both in mainland Europe and Britain, practicing Christians are few and getting fewer. I have heard statistics given of one in three in England believe in God, and only 6% in London attend church regularly. One primary reason given is the disillusionment and depersonalized psychic numbness cited earlier from two catastrophic wars on their soil. Both the fields of soldiers' anonymous, putrefying bodies and the Holocaust deny a just god's existence. Only in America do sizable numbers cling to an anthropomorphic, compassionate, omnipotent Being.

The more committed one is to a Savior-Rescuer and to achieving the requisite profile that will get one into Heaven, the more precipitous the loss of footing and greater the death anxiety may be if or when disillusionment begins unraveling the protective shield which that afterlife belief provided.

There are many other ironies and discrepancies between tenet and execution which have crept up in theistic religions in the course of delivering salvation from death and its fears.

IRONY 1. The Qur'an, the Holy Book of Islam, is considered to have greater historical authenticity than many other sacred books and writings in world religions because it had been fully recorded by Muhammad's aides a mere 18 years after his death.

Muhammad is not more than an Apostle; many were the Apostles that passed away before him. (3:144) We have sent thee inspiration, as We sent it to Noah and the Messengers after him: We sent inspiration to Abraham, Isma'il, Isaac, Jacob and the Tribes, to Jesus, Job, Jonah, Aaron, and Solomon, and to David We gave the Psalms. (4:163) Say: "We believe in Allah, and in what has been revealed to us and what was revealed to Abraham, Isma'il, Isaac, Jacob and the Tribes, and in (the Books) given to Moses, Jesus, and the Prophets, from their Lord: We make no distinction between one and another among them, and to Allah do we bow our will (in Islam)." (3:84) Those who believe (in the Qur'an), and those who follow the Jewish (scriptures), and the Christians and the Sabians, any who believe in Allah and the Last Day, and work righteousness, shall have their reward with their Lord; on them shall be no fear, nor shall they grieve. (2:62).[8]

Muhammad was far-sighted in his attitude towards the rights of women. His goal was to establish a society that took care of the downtrodden and poor. On the theistic side, though, the problem comes in with the Christian claim of Jesus being God-made-flesh. "Christ the son of Mary was no more than a messenger" (5:75).[9]

I certainly can understand how easily claims to Jesus' elevation to divinity and the Trinity can be perceived as arrogant and blasphemous. If we cannot see matters of faith and conscience through another's eyes, are we not doomed? Oil added to the fire, with governmental blame often deflected abroad, and cultural East-West clashes over the place of women and religion foretell a future of perilous uncertainty. It is a future far removed from Muhammad's enlightened ecumenism.

Just as Muhammad affirmed a single, even-handed God revealed through human voices to different cultures, the Hindus make a similar point in a marvelous Krishna story.

The tale relates how in the night Krishna the cowherd used to collect the milkmaids to dance with him in the forest. He would multiply himself in order to accommodate each of them. But at the moment each milkmaid, thinking this revered creator was hers alone, would jealously try to possess him, Krishna would vanish.

This game taught the milkmaids that God did not belong to any one of them but was nonpartisan. Jealous human need for superiority and exclusive possession was, and is, the problem.[10]

IRONY 2. Judaism has never had Christianity's afterlife focus. Hillel, who lived around the time of Jesus, was an eminent sage, interpreter of Torah and ultimately president of the Sanhedrin. A heathen came to him and vowed he would be converted if Hillel could teach him all the Torah while he stood on one leg. Hillel converted him with these words. "What is hateful to you, do not do to your fellow. That is all the Torah. The rest is commentary—go and study."[11]

As though in one voice with Hillel (and Confucius 600 years prior), Jesus gave an altered but no better version. The singular message is the same and a simple one focused on *this* life, not the next. Indeed, Judaism never had Christianity's prime focus on an afterlife, nor did Jesus!

BLACK IRONY 3. Odd about the fate of the Judeo part of the Judaic-Christian culture. Back in the really old days, the Yahweh of Abraham and Moses played favorites and performed favors, like the timely drowning of Egyptians in the Red Sea. By the sixth century, the Judaic concept of God had changed. Their God was no longer exclusive, but the loving and just God of all peoples. So what did the Jews get for sharing their Rescuer? The Holocaust.

This particular religious irony in the evolvement of monotheistic thought is a backdoor suggestion that another conceptual change is overdue in monotheistic religions. I do not believe a single homogenous faith is the answer, since unique religious traditions have been a wonderful, distinguishing, cultural heritage to honor and preserve. But deep, educated respect for other paths to God is critical.

No one was wiser or more prescient in this than Muhammad. And just as Muhammad embraced other faiths collectively under one God, so did Jesus and Hillel embrace the treatment and shared identity of all individuals belonging to all those faiths.

IRONY 4. There are three ways to approach Jesus in Western Christianity. The personal Jesus—a private, emotional relationship. The institutional Jesus—among like-minded believers; this includes the fundamentalist position that if the Bible says it, it is true—end of discussion. The historical Jesus—the man who emerges after an objective, scholarly search for what really happened.

Many scholars who have sought the historical truth of the man outside the mythic Biblical realm acknowledge the presence of primary components of the Jesus myth in the traditions and mystery cults of that time. Prominent among them, Mithraism was centered in Tarsus, Paul's hometown, and is the origin to which Reverend Davidson Loehr leans. "With the exception of the sayings attributed to Jesus, virtually everything now known as Christianity was probably taken from Mithraism. The cult of Mithras was the one-stop shop from which Christianity took its beliefs, sacraments, story, ecclesiology and salvation theme; its Pope and its headquarters on the Vatican Hill in Rome."[12]

Dr. Loehr points out that story elements—such as the Twelve Disciples, the Last Supper with the Twelve, Jesus' death as Savior of humans, the Ascension to Heaven, the Pope, December 25 as Jesus' birthday, and heaven, hell and purgatory awaiting us at death—all existed comparably within the Mithraic cult. Some were aspects in other cults as well and did not originate with Christianity. (The chicken or the egg question regarding resurrection themes in these cults is a stimulating one among historians, and unresolved.)

Who, then, do proponents of this liberal theology say Jesus was? For one thing, it is believed Jesus grew up in Galilee, melting pot and crossroads of various faiths, cultural backgrounds, customs and dietary laws. Also believed was that he was baffled that he and a potpourri of chums could not dine together. In essence to him, such barriers and distinctions were not of God. He taught his disciples that whether as beggars or guests in another's home, they were to eat whatever the host put before them, be it pork or potato.

The consensus of a group of highly credentialed religious academics, published scholars and clergy (popularly known as the Jesus Seminar), regarding lines *definitely* ascribable to Jesus, was that Jesus did not talk about his own divinity, bodily resurrection or an afterlife. His gaze was unflinchingly on one revolutionary message above all: To believe there was a difference between Roman and Jew—or (today) between Arab, Jew and Christian—and to identify oneself thusly was to be an enemy of the Kingdom. Jesus' mission was to "subvert exclusive identities." That message, Loehr states, "will get you shot any time, any place."

To "love thy neighbor" is a slam-dunk. To love and identify with thy enemies, that's something else. The religion *of* Jesus is too hard, and very few have practiced it. It is not for the weak or for those wanting mystery, miracle, magic and authority, Loehr observes. If all that the religion of Jesus is offering "is a better world filled with love, justice and compassion, gimme a break. I want a ride at the end!"[13]

As for the religion *about* Jesus, many scholars firmly hold that Christianity was created by Paul, his followers and the authors of the gospels and epistles. This brings up the question, if Jesus eschewed any group with an exclusive identity, would he be a Christian if he came back tomorrow? (Or would he look at the world mess and say, "I told you so. You still don't get it?") Would Muhammad be a Muslim? Would Buddha be a Buddhist? (How would this do for dinner party conversation?) Surely, Buddha would laugh at all the doctrines that bind us up!

About this, and close to verbatim, is a parable Dr. Loehr tells. There was once a time of terrible fighting and wars everywhere. Everyone was divided into tiny clubs, each one sure that only its members were right. They wanted other clubs to see that, too, and argued with them. But the other clubs never agreed, so there were horrible battles.

A young magician came to town. He didn't want to join a club, but he did amazing tricks.

Nobody wanted to hear him talk because he just made them mad. He told them that the reason they all fought was because they belonged to all the stupid clubs. "Get rid of them, and there will be no reason to fight," he told them. They thought this was ridiculous because their clubs were the only place they could find people who unquestionably were right also. They kept fighting and, although they loved the magician's tricks, they didn't pay much attention to what he said.

Then the young magician died, and a funny thing happened—although the magician would not have thought it funny. A new club started which was all about telling stories about what great tricks the magician had done.

This new club, in which members had to know and believe all the stories about what a great magician he had been, grew quickly because there had been some great tricks. It got so big, the club got an army. "Now we know how to end all the wars," the members said.

First, they went to all the meeting places where they had put statues and pictures of the magician and told the statues and pictures what they were going to do. Then they went out and fought a terrible war and won because they had the might and, of course, knew they were right. Many were forced to convert to their club.

The happy members went back to their meeting places to tell the statues and pictures of the magician what they had done. Afterwards, they turned out the lights and went off to drink and celebrate.

Then, the miracle happened! In all the meeting places everywhere, in the silence and darkness, all the statues and pictures began to cry.

Fantasyland? Check history for a multitude of parallel incredibilities. One, in 850 in Cordova, Spain, was started by a Christian monk named Perfectus. Under Muslim rule and until that time, Christians and Muslims got along nicely with broad religious tolerance and an advanced culture.

However, when Perfectus was asked by some Arabs who was the greater prophet, Muhammad or Jesus, the monk apparently "lost it." Instead of modestly answering in such a way as not to insult Muhammad, Perfectus let loose with invectives against Muhammad, including "sexual pervert" and "the Antichrist."

Authorities had no choice but to jail the priest.

The Qadi, the Islamic judge, wanted to believe Perfectus had been unreasonably provoked and gave him a second chance. When Perfectus snapped again, the Qadi had no choice but to execute him. A second monk followed suit with similar insults, and the reluctant Qadi again wanted to excuse him as drunk or crazy, but another round of insults to the Prophet followed; so, according to law, the second monk had to be executed also.

Naturally, some Christians saw this Get-the-Prophet demonstration as a Show-of-Faith bandwagon, and the fanatical rush to martyrdom continued. A ridiculous, fear-raising biography of Muhammad written in a monastery near Pamploma hadn't helped. In all, there were 50 "martyrs of Cordova," which were the last thing the Muslim powers wanted on their page in history.

Karen Armstrong notes that there was no law against proselytizing Christianity in the tolerant Islamic Empire as long as The Prophet was not maligned. The martyrs seemed to be searching for a Western identity in what was then a Muslim-dominated world. Armstrong makes the significant comparison that their loss of roots as a culture may have engendered the defiant religiosity in much the same way that the tables are reversed today and Western culture is perceived as threatening Muslim traditions and values.[14]

Finally, all sides returned to harmonious co-existence. No one knew to be grateful that they had lacked weapons of mass destruction.

There is indeed a strong case to be made against the motivational need of an afterlife and the divisive identities of competing, death-defying religions that were born to get you there. I would like to put on trial that cowardly Monster Worm, death anxiety, who started all this long ago. I want to hear the judge yell down at the sniveling Worm, "Nothingness is better than you deserve! Get a spine! Look at what the selfish, indulgent fear of dying has done to the world! Get over it!"

The irony must not be overlooked that James chose a worm eating away at each human core to be the metaphor for our deeply embedded fear of dying. Is not the worm ostensibly a *spineless* creature?

Beatle John Lennon wrote powerful lyrics for *Imagine*. He asks us to imagine that there is no religion, no countries for which to kill and die, nor possessions to breed hunger and greed, and that humankind is sharing this planet in peace. But before these, he asks us first to *imagine there is no heaven and there is no hell, and all Earth's people are living only for this moment, this day.*

---

[1] Aries, Philip. *Centuries of Childhood*. New York: Knopf, 1962, p. 36.
[2] Becker, Ernest. *Escape from Evil*. New York: Free Press, 1975.
[3] Primavesi, Anne. *Gaia's Gift: Earth, Ourselves, and God After Copernicus*. London: Routledge, 2003, p. 72.
[4] Nhât Hanh, Thich. *The Sun My Heart*. Berkeley: Parallax, 1988, p. 66.
[5] Kavanaugh, Robert E. *Facing Death*. Los Angeles: Nash, 1972, p. 220. (emphasis mine)
[6] Gandhi, Mahatma. "For the Well-being of the Nation." *The Message of Mahatma Gandhi*. U S Mohan Rao, ed. New Delhi: Ministry of Information and Broadcasting, 1968, pp. 90-92.
[7] Kastenbaum, Robert J., Ph.D. *Is There Life After Death? The Latest Evidence Analysed*. London: Prion, 1995, p. 258.
[8] Fisher, Mary Pat, and Lee W. Bailey. *An Anthology of Living Religions*. Upper Saddle River, NJ: Prentice-Hall, 2000, pp. 260-61.
[9] Ibid., p. 265.
[10] Eck, Diana L. *Encountering God: A Spiritual Journey from Bozeman to Banares*. Boston: Beacon Press, 1993, pp. 46-47.
[11] Fisher and Bailey. Op. cit., pp. 196-97.

12 Loehr, Davidson, Ph.D. Seminar. "Jesus: The Origins of Christianity and the Implications of 'Demythologizing' Western Religions." Oak Ridge, TN: Unitarian Universalist Church. 15-17 March 2002.
13 Ibid.
14 Armstrong, Karen. *Muhammad: A Biography of the Prophet*. San Francisco: Harper-Collins, 1993, pp. 21-25.

Chapter 10

The Pros of an Afterlife Belief

> *Religion solves the problem of death, which no living individuals can....Religion takes one's very creatureliness, one's insignificance, and makes it a condition of hope. Not as practiced, but as an ideal for mental health, Christianity, on all the things we have listed, stands high, perhaps even highest in some vital ways.*
>
> —Ernest Becker (1973)[1]

In the United States organized religion and the fear of death are entwined by a much larger margin of the population than elsewhere in Western society. America shows uniquely resilient strength among Western countries to hold onto an anthropomorphic Being with human characteristics of love, forgiveness and reward for good behavior. A significant percentage in Britain and Europe were unable to square a Being of compassion and omnipotence with two world wars and the Holocaust.

Whenever one group believes God is on its side of an issue and tragedy and death for others result, responsibility for that belief has to be assumed, as well as for the exclusive identity of the supporting religious ethos. The previous chapter addressed this subject, which would seem ridiculous to earlier generations and superfluous to individual death anxiety. After all, Americans' optimistic afterlife belief and the positive historical turnaround in the 20th-century medical community brought this country to *generally*[2] improved circumstances for dying as the millenium began. But September 11, 2001, symbolized change and lost innocence. A global clash of cultures and afterlife religions have brought us into uncharted territory in history.

We cannot fathom what story will come out of the opposing religious and cultural divisions. Respect and understanding of the other's core beliefs are essential for survival in a world weaponized for mass annihilation. If *any* group majority is going to use a system of religious beliefs as a chief defense against death anxiety, then it must not be blind to all the consequences of that exclusive identity system which uses God in its defense for war.

From this precarious position in which the world is struggling, the preceding chapter reminds that there is an underbelly to what U.S. polls indicate is the majority's best medicine for death anxiety.

But what does mass suffering throughout history have to do with the anxiety relief felt by the individual American believer-in-the-street as he or she ages and a natural terminal period arrives?

Almost nothing.

The Death of Ellen Augusta

She died a month ago in her hometown of Minneapolis. Her son is a friend of mine, and I was privileged to also know his mother for some years. Remarkably sharp, mentally well-groomed and with an exquisitely bright personality, she appreciated humor and gave it back. At 91, Ellen never appeared to notice the admiring glances her lovely face and figure attracted.

She had been a witness to the Lord all her life. Along with thoughtful acts of kindness toward those in her path, she was deeply committed to her husband and family. She had mentioned often in the past years how tired she was getting and how much she looked forward to being with her deceased husband.

My friend always replied there was too much in the coming weeks that they had to do together.

On a Monday, Ellen began to lose her appetite and by Thursday was feeling nauseated. She never experienced great pain. On Friday, her concerned family took her to the hospital. A viral infection was discovered, and she was fully medicated for pain and nausea. She remained alert as her vital functions steadily deteriorated.

Later that night, her large family circled the bed as my friend relived special memories with his mother. Finally, he leaned over and told his mom it was okay to go and join Pop. I understand it was not more than ten seconds later that the monitors went flat. Ellen died as she had lived, totally devoid of any fear of death.

A young girl, who worked in Ellen's apartment house and with whom she had prayed daily, cried inconsolably when she came to work the following morning. She grieved her own loss of a great friend who had been and would continue to be an exemplary Christian role model to follow. Ellen's memory and legacy would reach long into the future, extend far beyond her immediate family.

The traditional Christian faith with its promise of the forgiveness of sins is strong medicine for death anxiety. The many who share Ellen's faith and have lived accordingly fear no evil as they walk on the ground of those beliefs through the valley of death's shadow. Certainly, good afterlife theology and close family support is the American "way to go."

Atchley's *Social Forces of Aging* juxtaposes Koenig's findings that uncertain and sporadically religious people show the most death fears, with Kalish's own supporting research that strongly religious believers and affirmed atheists show few death fears.[3] In my research, these are among the most important findings to ponder, to weigh in the context of one's own fears. When it comes to religious belief and the afterlife, it doesn't pay to be on the fence.

Some pros

A number of bright lights in the history of religions also stand out to their credit. Six thousand years ago, the Egyptians possessed a religion and system of morality equal to any before or since. Immortality was an axiom in the Egyptian mind from the first burial, just as it was a universal belief in all savage, primitive races. Under polytheistic beliefs at times, still there was never an Egyptian period without the concept of one creator god, immortal, omnipotent, invisible.

The earliest burials were in the embryonic position, as the American Hopi Indian custom was, for example, as if in preparation for rebirth. The Egyptians were the first people to conceive the idea that a man's ethical conduct in life determined his post-mortem destiny. This was a landmark in the history of ethics, according to famed Egyptologist Sir Wallis Budge. Weighed on the scales of virtue, one could be brought back to life by the power of Osiris, conqueror of death and bestower of a resurrection.[4]

Another bright historical light shines amid the tragedy of a lack of a global religious vocabulary. It is the Sufi example, the mystical arm of Islam. Since its inception around the ninth century, the movement has sought a return to simplicity and the interior state of Muhammad when he received the revelations.

Armstrong notes that Sufis went back to the Qur'an's spirit of inclusive appreciation of other religions. For example, some "were especially devoted to Jesus [as a human Prophet], whom they saw as the ideal Sufi since he preached a gospel of love."[5] Unfettered, ecstatic expression was characteristic of the "drunken Sufis," such as that of the early Sufi mystic Al-

Bistami. He practiced the discipline of *fanah* (annihilation) "*by gradually peeling away the layers of egotism (which, all spiritual writers agree, holds us back from the experience of the divine)*" in order to sense a transcending spiritual connection within his own being.[6] The great poet and writer of Sufi scripture, Rumi was also a "drunken Sufi" and the founder of the trance-inducing "Whirling Dervishes." He likewise taught that one must conquer the illusions of the ego and, in essence, feel at home with the divine whether in a mosque or synagogue.

Sounds like the Nazarene carpenter to me.

Here is a back door "pro" for staying dead when dead, whether there is an afterlife or not! Eugene Paul Wigner won the 1963 Nobel Prize in Physics and numerous other prestigious awards and honors. In an interview with Goodman, he revealed his intense love of his family and his "work for its own sake, not because I believe it's important." Asked whether he would choose to come back for a short time after his death—any time from between two to 1000 years, he immediately replied emphatically, "Not at all." Why not? "I am worried about what I would see. It could be sad."[7]

Is there an afterlife? The answer is: Some form of survival cannot be disproved. For every argument that has been tried, there is a counter-argument. Following are a few examples which fall in the middle or lean to the affirmative.

Presenting the biological argument, David Lund agrees that the theory of the brain as producer of consciousness is more plausible, but is not more provable, than the theory which proposes that the brain functions rather like a transmitter or receiver of consciousness. When the brain is injured, or physical sense or speech organs impaired or destroyed, consciousness would be "disembodied" and would be unable to make its existence known by the given bodily channels. Thus, transactions between the "two worlds"—the flow of consciousness—would be impeded the least by an alert, healthy brain and affected the most by a stroke.

According to this theory, the origin of consciousness exists independently of the brain. Lund concluded the source could be either a "single cosmic consciousness or else there is a source of consciousness corresponding to each of us" (he calls the latter the transcendental source within). *The latter is where the paranormal phenomena come in as support for the transmission theory and other survival views.*[8]

Aldous Huxley's theory in his influential *Doors of Perception* derived from his experiences under the influence of mescaline. He believed the brain and nervous system act as a "central reducing valve" through which (otherwise overwhelming) all-knowing "Mind at Large" is channeled. This consciousness really is a survival mechanism which allows only the information through that will allow the person to win the fight for survival. Some, such as mystics and psychics, are born with a "bypass" around their reducing valve, and others have a temporary access to "Mind at Large" through spiritual exercises, yoga and certain drugs.

Lund finds Huxley's work also supportive of the selective transmission theory in regard to the so-called near-death experiences, or out-of-body experiences, in which extraordinary experiences come when the oxygen supply to the brain is deprived. Furthermore, Lund points out, if no differences have been found between brain nerve cells and those in the spinal cord, and they are notably similar to all other cells in chemical composition and structure, then how, he questions, can these very ordinary cells *generate* conscious experience?

A glimmer of hope for not just an afterlife but a positive one, comes from D. Barrett's study of death dreams. Compiled from the dream diaries of around 1,200 young adults in good health, results showed that dreams about one's actual dying and death have a pleasant, peaceful quality by a huge margin; none were checked as unpleasant. Of the two dream varieties reported, neither had a negative connotation, and the more prevalent type involved going on to an afterlife experience. In the other dream type, death came like a quiet, peaceful fainting. I had one dream exactly like this, my breath slowing down and stopping—an entirely serene process. But dreams of almost dying were reported as uncomfortable episodes.[9]

Death dreams can represent transformation in life. However, Barrett's study also brings to mind the glowing reports of near-death experiences, which suggests these NDE's may be indeed reports of returns from actual passages into death as opposed to being experiences of people *almost* dying.

All *psychic phenomena* point to an afterlife where either one returns to this realm or exists in another. These are placed in the "pro" column because, on the whole, a belief in any of them theoretically can have a positive, humanitarian effect.

The minor exceptions of the caste system in India and the historically passive acceptance of suffering in both Hinduism and Buddhism are giving way to proactive compassion in both, which is more the norm today. It still holds that both Buddha and modern Ghandi preached non-violence and compassion as responses to aggression, an improvement, some say, to the policy of retaliation.

Especially positive humanitarian effects are in the reincarnation area in Kastenbaum's view. He gives a delightful list of reasons why the meaning of life for a reincarnate has relatively more salubrious consequences.

Reincarnates have a deeper sense of contact to the past and relationship with the well-being of others, including animals. Moreover, they feel a responsibility for the future and have a vested interest in improving earthly life for generations to come, including means for their own karmic advancement. The concept of sin, all but unknown in cultures such as Buddhism, is replaced by one of a spiritual quest. There is no fixed identity in reincarnate thinking. Change is constant. Rigid *do*'s and *don't*'s, handed down by a father judge to become locked into an immature model, are replaced by the release of oneself to the awesome mysteries of the universe.

In short, says Kastenbaum, "reincarnates may well be more pleasant people to have around: sensitive, responsible, attuned to the larger picture, not consumed by pride and anxiety and not welded to a juvenile conception of deity, and not casually destructive of life on earth."[10]

To this I add my own thought regarding both the concept of afterlife in general and the karmic perspective of reincarnation in particular. Namely, given that the physical principles of the universe have such purpose and sense-making to them, it makes no sense to have a species gain steadily in wisdom and knowledge over a lifetime only to have that progression be for naught.

Psychic Phenomena: A Bottom Line

Certain books have stood out in my research. Edwin Shneidman's *Voices of Death* won my vote as "most moving and meaningful" and is as timely and on target today as when it was published in 1980. For "outstanding title" *Death as a Career Move* won, hands down. I guessed it would be a how-to on funeral-home management or even grave-digging opportunities. But no! It was mystery fiction. For "most interesting and entertaining" Kastenbaum's *Is There Life After Death?* took the honors. For "most impressive documentation and erudite footnotes," many of which were classical text sources, Jan Bremmer's *The Rise and Fall of the Afterlife* was without parallel. The two latter were invaluable in separating wheat from chaff in the area of the paranormal.

"Psychic" means "pertaining to the soul, not physical." Webster's defines a psychic as "one sensitive to nonphysical forces," and psychical research as "an investigation into phenomena that appear contrary to physical laws and suggest possibility of mental activity apart from the body." The principal phenomena are the out-of-body experience (near-death experiences are among these), the death-bed escort, poltergeists, the medium and reincarnation.

Another, the *psychomanteum*, or apparition chamber, is the recent study of Dr. Raymond Moody, Jr., known for his in-depth study of the near-death experience. The only required element is a reflective surface into which the seeker gazes.

Dating back to classical times and the famed Oracle of the Dead at Ephyra, a divination mirror apparently was used by the Aztecs as well. Kastenbaum reports Moody's study of the Elizabethan scholar John Dee who uncovered the Aztec practice. Dee found he could see visions in a mirror as well, and the Queen even visited his home to observe these phenomena for herself. In those days, acceptance of the spirit world was more natural.

Moody replicated a contemporary version and had positive feedback from normal, everyday people who sensed the real presence of deceased loved ones. Nothing conclusive can be said except that the experience eases the pain of many grief-stricken relatives and friends.

Mention can be made of *poltergeists*, or ghosts, if only to conclude a large number which have not been proved fraudulent have particular predispositions. Kastenbaum states these as emotional instability, intense stress and a proclivity to dissociative reactions.[11] As for the remaining cases, none had either applied or passed the rigorous study controls needed for verification.

F.W.H. Myers, one of the founders of the investigative British Society of Psychical Research in 1882, stated a better explanation for ghosts is an "afterimage" or residue, similar to the bright light that remains often after we close our eyes. It entails "the perceiver's reaction to a stimulus generated by something that has already disappeared or changed."[12]

The foci with the *medium* are automatic writing and trance reception. Myers himself provided skeptics one of the most stupefying cases of afterlife to this day. He looked forward to the time death provided the answer at last to his quest on earth. If there were an afterlife, he was determined to transmit conclusive proof to the living by the method known as "cross-correspondences."

After his death, Myers communicated pieces of complex verbal puzzles through automatic writing to each of a number of mediums. They then had to get together to discover Myers' perfect, complete message to them! These messages were far too complicated to synopsize in a short space as they were often filled with complicated literary allusions interwoven among them to perhaps seven recipients. In addition, Myers could observe the living and clarify telepathic messages between them!

Furthermore, Kastenbaum notes Myers was the exception to a number of charges of fraud against mediumship. Namely, even if these spirits do survive temporarily, they fade away or die again rapidly. This is a blessing normally, since they are reduced to idiots, making fools of themselves in dumb, trivial speech. However, Myers' I.Q. never diminished in his intricate network of cross-correspondences, which lasted approximately 30 years.

A favorite example of mine is again from early in the last century. I believe it, along with that of Myers' survival experiment, surpasses cases offered today in aspects which have a measure of verification.

Eileen Garrett was a British author and an executive, among other credits. Not only was she reticent to display her psychic gifts, she also was an exception to the rule in that, unlike other mediums, she did not believe particularly in an afterlife. She helped to fund strict scientific investigations of the field and of her own remarkable abilities in it.

In this instance, in 1930, Eileen Garrett had begun her trance when an unexpected, unknown voice came through her. He identified himself as Flight Lieutenant H. Carmichael Irwin and proceeded to give an anguished running description of the failure of mechanical equipment on some sort of air vehicle. He expressed an urgent need to communicate the reasons for it. His retrospective account ended with the prediction of the structural engineering problems that would be given as cause at an enquiry to be held in the future.

As it turned out, the famed British dirigible R101 with Irwin as its commanding officer had crashed just two days prior to Garrett's session. At that time, no one but the dead Irwin could have known the technical information he imparted during Garrett's trance. Of further intrigue, a British aviation investigator, Major Villiers, communicated with other witnesses, including receiving detailed testimony from another crew member. No details that Irwin conveyed to Garrett were found to be incorrect in the subsequent official inquiry.

The *death-bed escort* is easily overlooked here in the connection to the near-death experience. A welcoming escort or apparition appears to the dying person. In both situations, is the cause biochemical or supernatural? Unlike the near-death experience, apparitions can appear to those clear of mind and not thought by some to be in grave danger—yet who die shortly thereafter. Fairly rare, these escorts are varied, such as a parent, an angel and so on. Many who have witnessed such death-bed visions, Kastenbaum among them, have been impressed and left wondering. However, like the psychomanteum, the death-bed escort is easier to accept as wish-fulfillment.

Has anything changed in the last 2500 years of ghosts, conjurers and staring into mirrors? A comparison between the 21st century and classical examples from the 5th century B.C. in Greece and Rome is enlightening!

Early Greeks were less concerned with personal survival and more concerned with collective, social survival. Eventually, in the Archaic Age inscriptions on graves in remembrance of individuals began to appear. The cultural perspectives in play today between collective versus an ego orientation have much precedent. When the individual takes the stage, an anxious desire for personal death exemption becomes pressing!

There were, of course, the Eleusinian Mysteries. Then, there were the Pythagoreans and Orphism, which Bremmer singles out as the two sects offering doctrines of an afterlife. The movements formed under Pythagoras and the figurehead of the mythical poet Orpheus during the fifth century B.C. in Greece as well as likely in southern Italy and Sicily. The former was focused more on history and ethics, and the latter on mythology and purifications since Orphism, of the two, embodied a sense of guilt. Given the focus on reincarnation, some form of vegetarianism was likely.

Among the plethora of examples Bremmer offers, here are two. Xenophanes reports that Pythagoras saw a dog being beaten and told the abuser to quit. Evidently, in hearing the dog's "voice," he recognized the soul of a friend in the canine.[13]

The second involves Hermotimos of Klazomenai. It was said that his soul would take off for years and appear in different places to foretell the future. Finally, it would re-enter his body back home "as into a sheath." Ultimately, his wife betrayed him, and his enemies burned his stiff body in order to make it impossible for his soul to reclaim it after the current trip. "The inhabitants of Klazomenai felt they had to atone for this crime, and they founded a sanctuary for the heroized Hermotimos from which women, naturally, are excluded till the present day."[14] And although Bremmer discredits the sources of the story, it is a great one!

Around this time the Greek idea developed that the dead were materially better off, and Orphics conceived of hell as a place where sinners wallowed around in mud. Around 432 B.C. the concept that afterlife was not subterranean, but rather celestial had arrived. However, despite "the symposium of the pure" fostered in Pythagorean and Orphic circles, both Greek drama and Plato evince that the majority of Greeks did not believe in rewards and punishments after death. They had no expectations. "In Plato's *Phaedo*, Simmias even claims that it is the fear of the majority that their soul is scattered at death 'and this is their end'."[15]

Consulting the dead through conjurers, or mediums, has long been a universal practice. In Book 11 of the *Odyssey*, Odysseus goes to the underworld to consult Tiresias. In Greece, the inquirer would be lowered into a crypt, by cranes supposedly, to hang out below for weeks. At that point, having visions and hearing voices would be reasonable expectations!

Plato abhorred all of this. In his *Laws* (10, 909B), he suggested a life of solitary confinement for those who "fool many of the living by pretending to raise the dead." Bremmer notes that the aversion extended to Rome's upper classes, where such connections were considered the lowest form of trickery. But necromancy retained a measure of popularity nevertheless.

One recalls Saul asking an old woman diviner to consult the dead King Samuel (I Samuel 28), who accurately foretold Saul's and his sons' deaths. Also, there is "The publication in 1966 of a reconstructed Jewish handbook on magic which probably dates to the early fourth century....The magical material is clearly older, even provides detailed instructions for the questioning of a ghost and speaking with spirits."[16] The conclusion after 2500 years is that the more things change, the more they remain the same in human nature and needs.

The two remaining phenomena, reincarnation and the near-death experience, have both born the scrutiny of recent, demanding collars and controls put in place by highly credentialed academics and clinicians.

The *near-death experience* of those in a close call with death or without a quantitative heartbeat has three dimensions: mystical, depersonalization and hyper-alertness. Common characteristics reported upon resuscitation are separation from the body, movement upward (frequently passing through a tunnel), a sense of a different world, usually meeting others known to the person, often a rapid non-judgmental life review with another being there, calm and peace, and a moment of decision to stay or go back towards the end of the experience. Above all and invariably is the intense, bright light, warm and peaceful, either suffusing the scene or possibly emanating from a Being.

Importantly, returned to life, there is a profound and spiritual change of attitudes and life, including an absence of any future fear of death and the realization of more concern for others.

Children do not report a life review or meeting with relatives. There is no report of a tunnel in experiences recounted in India and China. Could the factor here be the Western appropriation of "the light at the end of the tunnel" and the relief felt when it is glimpsed?

Bremmer states there are five cases in classical literature which some might call NDE. "On the Delays of the Divine Vengeance," found in Plutarch's *Moralia*, was written sometime after 81 A.D. Thespesius and his guide are "shown how artisans hammered souls into shape for their rebirth." [17] Bremmer says that this, as in other classical examples, was a composite, written to express a philosophical or ethical position rather than a genuine NDE. Excepted, however, he notes, are the feeling of drifting upward and recognition of former friends. Also, Thespesius came back totally changed and reformed. Compared to modern accounts, medieval accounts lack a feeling of peace, a life review, the tunnel, hovering above the body and meeting with deceased relatives. Bremmer suggests this might indicate that relationships were emotionally cold and distant within the monastery from which most came. Different and noteworthy are the detailed descriptions and focus on even tiny sins.

The primary experience can occur sometimes when there is no peril of bodily death and is called an out-of-body experience, or OBE. Many highly skilled researchers have looked into and written about the OBE and NDE. Names such as Greyson, Ring, Moody, Sabom and Morse are well-respected in the academic and popular marketplace. One whose early work and case-study methods are lauded among his peers is Dr. Michael Sabom, a cardiologist who confirmed the visual accuracy of emergency room descriptions among those resuscitated who reported NDEs.

Nuland holds that the NDE is the effect of several million years of evolution. Among the probable causes, he joins others in naming endorphins or similarly the defense mechanism known as depersonalization, seizures in the brain's temporal lobes, inadequate oxygenation of the brain or the effects of narcotics such as those given in cases of lingering deaths. In short, Nuland sees a biochemical explanation likely for this phenomenon.[18]

Quite recent findings shed a much stronger light on the temporal lobe theory. A research report published in 2004 found that, contrary to expectations, people who have these experiences have excellent take-charge coping skills under stress. They sleep an hour less and move more slowly into the REM (Rapid Eye Movement) phase of sleep.

Highly significant was the correlation of the experience to epileptiform activity lateralized in the left hemisphere of the brain, rather than the right, as expected. "These results suggest that altered temporal lobe functioning may be involved in the near-death experience and that individuals who have had such experiences are physiologically distinct from the general population....[These findings] are not consistent with post-traumatic symptomology. However, they may be indicative of a pre-existing condition that predisposes individuals to unusual reactions to acute stress."[19]

Cause or result is the question, then. Based on certain factors, Britton and Bootzin tend to believe that the temporal lobe and sleep findings in the NDE group are not a "generalized result of trauma, [but rather] specific to the near-death experience itself."[20] The specific events of participants in their study were predominently accidents, then medical complications and heart attacks, then allergic reactions and suicide attempts.

Another well-known name in the field, Dr. C. Bruce Greyson, a psychiatrist at the University of Virginia, has found similar, positive, coping patterns in his studies, with hardly any indication of blocking reality, a condition known as dissociation. He states from 9 to 18 percent of those who have nearly died later report having experienced this phenomenon. "Dr. Greyson theorizes that the experience may be a protective mechanism that insulates some people against developing post-traumatic stress disorder."[21] Regarding the cause-and-effect question again, whether or not the findings were pre-existing characteristics or the result of the NDE is the subject of a study Greyson has recently undertaken.

As to *reincarnation*, Voltaire was of this opinion: "After all, it is no more surprising to be born twice than to be born once."

The man who holds the key to the afterlife question has stated, "I believe that everyone should examine the evidence for reincarnation for himself and make up his own mind." On another occasion he remarked, "There is an impressive body of evidence, and it is getting stronger all the time. I think a rational person, if he wants, can believe in reincarnation on the basis of evidence."[22] The man quoted here is Dr. Ian Stevenson, Research Professor of Psychiatry at the University of Virginia who for many decades has been the finest clinical researcher in this field.

The scientific controls and collars he placed on over 3,000 case studies are acclaimed among peers. An objective researcher and academic, he shuns the spotlight and popular marketplace, refusing media and magazine interviews. He writes only for the academic and scientific community, although Tom Shroder wrote a fascinating book about his travels with Stevenson, *Old Souls: The Scientific Search for Proof of Past Lives*.

His casework in India, Thailand, Sri Lanka, Lebanon, Turkey, Thailand and Burma centered on children. A typical case usually starts between age two and four with the child's descriptions of previous lives, accompanied by unexpected behavior. At age five to six, he or she starts to forget and talks less about them.

Of interest to me is the tendency for a violent death to have ended the child's recalled lifetime. I wonder if there is some sort of better karmic future and return planned for those who are victims of premature death. Or, I wonder if reincarnation is quite common, or even universal, but only those who died in an *intensely* traumatic and *memorable* way are able to retain that memory through the transition simply because of its extraordinary nature.

Of course, Vergil and Plato had an intellectual explanation that appealed to the reasoning of classical philosophers. When souls are about to be reincarnated, they are compelled to drink of the waters of forgetfulness and thus cannot remember their past lives. Again, though, the imprint may be so strong from violent death or impressionable previous life circumstances that it remains.

The subject of many of Stevenson's more recent and massive evidential files is a physical mark or deformity which corresponds exactly to a wound, usually mortal, or a scar on the person the child recalls being. His scholarly *When Reincarnation and Biology Intersect* was published by Praeger Press in 1997. It is a summary of *Reincarnation and Biology: A Contribution to the Etiology of Birthmarks and Birth Defects*, available in two volumes and 2,000-plus pages. Earlier works, *Children Who Remember Past Lives: A Question of Reincarnation* (1987) and *Twenty Cases Suggestive of Reincarnation* (1974) should be in libraries, certainly university ones. I sat at one, pouring over Stevenson's other magnum opus, *Cases of the Reincarnation Type* (1975-83). These four huge volumes have the call number BL515S746 and are owned by most academic institutions. In them and others cited, evidence awaits anyone curious about an afterlife.

He has published a number of academic papers and articles on *xenoglossy* in his cases. *Xenoglossy* is the ability to speak or write in a language of which the speaker has absolutely no experience. However, it appears Stevenson's evolved focus has been the connection of physical birthmarks and defects journeying from one alleged incarnation to another. The stories attached to them have been methodically corroborated and are accompanied by hard documentation, such as photographs.

One case concerned Ravi Shankar, who remembered being decapitated by two people. One of the murderers was a relative who wanted to inherit Ravi's father's wealth. Around his neck Ravi had a linear mark that looked like the scar caused by a knife.

Another case described in a presentation by Stevenson involved a child in Turkey who remembered a life as a bandit. Rather than be captured, he committed suicide by placing a gun under the right side of his chin. This child was born with an horrific gash under his chin. An elderly man was able to confirm to Stevenson seeing both the bandit's death and the condition of the body. Stevenson figured out that the wound would have had to create an exit hole in the brain area. Upon examination, there was indeed another scar a bit left of the crown. On a slide, both scars were pictured clearly in a direct line of trajectory that the bullet would have taken, and the alignment was perfectly matched. If such a wound had occurred in the boy's current lifetime, he would not be around to talk about it!

Stevenson has written that he is now suspicious of any subject who claims to have been shot or stabbed in a previous lifetime if there are no corresponding marks on the body. Perhaps, he has suggested, there is some kind of non-physical body unknown to us which carries such imprints between lifetimes.[23] Also, many of his cases have involved the recall of previous spouses. Not only is the child able to identify them visually and by name, as well as other relatives, frequently the child reveals sordid or "uncomfortable" truths which would have been known only to the two of them. One former wife fainted dead away in embarrassment.

An open mind? Kastenbaum concludes that the orthodox view of death cannot accommodate these phenomena. How can only one be reincarnated unless all are, he asks. He points out that if we really had an open mind to the huge accumulation of reported phenomena, we might find only one conclusion possible—that death is not the same for everybody! Naturally, no one can open his or her eyes that wide and objectively, or else they might come to what Kastenbaum calls the idea of pluralistic death![24]

Could the ultimate challenge be the concept of death as a variable? Of course, the variable is in the possibilities that might be open once bodily functions have ceased. The interesting aspect of this entertaining phrase "pluralistic death" was the very different interpretation given to it by two men, both eminent in their fields.

One, a well-known, widely published critic and author of both fiction and nonfiction, responded instantly that of course there are many deaths in life. Analogous to Lifton's symbolic modes and Capra's film examples, his interpretation is revealing of a highly accomplished, creative person's sense of constant renewal with each work.

With every completion comes a feeling of loss, then a new creative incubation and regeneration begins again. This writer, though, was referring to the various types of losses we all sustain. Some can be devastating and cause partial death, a permanent deadening of emotional arteries. Others are analogous to letting go of the monotone rhythm of one trapeze and taking the risk that the next trapeze will be there to carry you forward when you turn. Whatever necessitates the turn, whether one's own decision to slough off a false identity or another's doing, such as can occur in a divorce or lost job, it holds the potential of a passage from a death to a rebirth.

I have found striking the number of times "death" and "growth" are linked together on paper, and I am becoming programmed to presume that physical death must be filled with the same potential for opportunity!

The British Society of Psychical Research

Returning to the unnerving term "pluralistic death" for its second interpretation, I went to the British Society for Psychical Research.[25] The afternoon I spent there with Nicholas Clarke-Howes was spiritually helpful to me and my baggage of Western logic.

Clarke-Howes held a Doctorate of Theology and was the esteemed Librarian of the Society, whose purpose has been investigation, not promotion, of psychic phenomena. He chose his responses carefully, stressing that while numerous people support the given view, others do not.

Of psychic phenomena, 95% are mental, that is, comprised of spiritual, visual images, while 5% are physical, such as actual photographs of ghosts.

Do different phenomena tend to happen to the same people, that is, is a medium, for example, more susceptible to an out-of-body experience as well? Clarke-Howes' simple answer I believe to be *a comprehensive key to unlocking some understanding of this entire subject.*

All these experiences come *while one is in an altered state,* when the barrier is down between consciousness and unconsciousness. Although such experiences usually occur unexpectedly, the recipient must be conducive to a belief in such phenomena. *Some people are simply able to accept and lower the barrier more easily than others.*[26]

In Elizabethan England, communion with the spirit world was quite common and accepted. It appears the scientific age has intervened and thrown up mental barriers in many minds. (I would note here that numerous children in cultures, such as the Hindu in India, recalling past lives spontaneously is understandable because, where the threshold is down for reincarnation belief, the memory comes naturally.)

Regarding *mediumship* and *channeling,* Clarke-Howes reiterated that it *occurs only when everyone involved is receptive.* Three possibilities exist about the source of the information being gathered: 1) the spirit of the departed, 2) extrasensory perception from the "sitter" who knew the departed, 3) from the "cosmic memory bank." Current opinion appears to be coming down on the side of survival rather than super-ESP or cosmic memory.

Presented with the phrase "pluralistic death," Clarke-Howes smiled appreciative recognition. He said many believe that there is a second death, or "moving on," of the spirit-personality to a third life, in unity perhaps with God or the source of life.

Among the support for this is the inability of mediums to communicate with the departed for more than a very approximate two years *or* for more time than the memory of the deceased is held fresh by those left behind. It is a finite period, ended when the departed is suddenly forever cut off from the reach of the medium (who usually never knew the subject alive). The implication is an apparent moving on to another plateau.

I propose maybe we get what we think we will! Or perhaps the circumstances at death—*or* the cosmic forces such as govern astrology and the concept of yin and yang at the time of death—*or* even the person's age, millennium and shifting changes in the universe determine the afterlife fate. Does not the age of quantum physics and the "black hole" theory embolden this mental stretch?

Perhaps the entertaining way to remember death as a variable is as a shell game. What's behind Door One? Door Two? Door Three? Or what's above Floor One? Floor Two? Floor Three? However, time spent wondering whether your beautiful, spiritual body is issued filmy white fatigues or whether bleached blondes end up natural or as blondes has a minus factor on any scale.

At a three-day conference in New York City, I sat one seat away from Karen Armstrong. During a conversation on one of our breaks, I asked her a question about two opposing views on a minor aspect of Buddhism's reincarnate belief. She ended her response with, "You know what the Buddha would have said? 'If it helps you on your path to believe in reincarnation, then do. If it doesn't help you, then forget it'."[27] And she was so right, as the Buddha would have been.

What is important are the polls.

Harris Poll collected the following data from 2,201 participants out of the general American population during the week of 21-27 January 2003. The margin of error is only 2%.[28]

Respondents	By	age	Overall
Who Believe In:	64 +	25-29	
Reincarnation	14%	40%	27%
Ghosts	27%	65%	51%
Accuracy of Astrology	17%	43%	31%

In one generation Americans have moved by a huge percentage to a different understanding of afterlife, one which returns a person to Earth in a new human form rather than having it remain in "heaven" and one in which a person from a former existence is easily accessible as a ghost. The implications of this trend on death attitudes and fears are enormous.

Regarding the accuracy of astrology, of interest here is the opinion Clarke-Howes shared when I asked about astrology and other ancient fortune-telling methods, such as the *I Ching*. He drew an analogy to findings that show a connection between power lines and discernible mental or emotional disturbance in those living underneath them. Cosmic forces with their definite rhythms and cycles of change introduce the questions of pre-cognition and a pre-ordained destiny.

Clarke-Howes brought up Rupert Sheldrake's opinion— that we set our own course quite early through the establishment of childhood habits. Significant was his statement addressing all these, that it is possible to change one's course once in motion, but it is not an easy task. These polls show an average of three out of ten more mindsets being tuned to different channels than those of the previous generation in matters of free will and afterlife.

Conclusion

The previous chapter looked at all the suffering that has been caused since recorded time by the human need to somehow continue and not be extinguished. This chapter points out that, in spite of all the suffering which has been caused by the human thirst to continue, all that matters is one person's fear of death. And for that, a belief in an afterlife can be a potent antidote. There are exceptions of course. Murderers and rapists might well vote for nothingness, and those who are victims of bad theology will unlikely be totally comfortable either while living or while dying. And those with low self-esteem, whether they are products of good theology or not, are going to have a tough time any way you cut it.

This chapter also addressed the credibility of specific psychic phenomena, which brings the discussion back to the ultimate question: Is there an afterlife?

The question, "Is there a God?" is easier to punt with the answer which I believe again can be credited to William James, Harvard's renowned psychologist and professor of philosophy of a century ago, who has been quoted throughout this text. God may not be true, he pointed out, but God is real because God has real effects. As we have seen, these effects have been both for the better and for the worse.

As for "Is there *proof* of an afterlife?" there might be an answer if an open mind were possible, because it takes only one irrefutable case study to prove an afterlife—perhaps an afterlife not for everyone, but an afterlife proved for that case study.

Each person must determine the answer based on the evidence as he or she evaluates it. A good place to start may be in a university library's card catalog under STEVENSON, IAN.

---

[1] Becker, Ernest. *The Denial of Death*. New York: Free Press, 1973, pp. 203-204.

[2] Notwithstanding the ravages of AIDS, poverty with uninsured health and higher incidence of fatal violence not related to a banner cause.

[3] Atchley, Robert C. *Social Forces of Aging*. Belmont, CA: Wadsworth Thomson Learning, 2000, p. 312.

[4] Budge, Sir E.A. Wallis. *The Book of the Dead: With a New Introduction by David Lorimer*. London: Arkana, 1985, and Budge, *Egyptian Religion: Egyptian Ideas of the Future Life*. London: Arkana, 1987.

[5] Armstrong, Karen. *Islam: A Short History.* New York: Modern Library, 2000, p. 74.
[6] Ibid., p. 75. (emphasis mine)
[7] Goodman, Lisl Marlburg, Dr. *Death and the Creative Life.* New York: Springer, 1981, pp. 83-87.
[8] Lund, David H. *Death and Consciousness.* Jefferson, NC: McFarland, 1985. (emphasis mine)
[9] Barrett, Deirdre. "Dreams of Death." *Omega: Journal of Death and Dying.* Robert J. Kastenbaum, Ph.D., ed. Farmingdale, NY: Baywood. 19.1 (1988-89): 95-103.
[10] Kastenbaum, Robert J., Ph.D. *Is There Life After Death?: The Latest Evidence Analysed.* Rev. Ed. London: Prion, 1995, pp. 188-89.
[11] Ibid., p. 123.
[12] Ibid., p. 128.
[13] Bremmer, Jan N. *The Rise and Fall of the Afterlife.* New York: Routledge, 2002, p. 12.
[14] Ibid., p. 39.
[15] Ibid., pp. 6-7.
[16] Ibid., p. 80
[17] Ibid., p. 94.
[18] Nuland, Sherwin. *How We Die.* New York: Knopf, 1994, pp. 138-39.
[19] Britton, Willoughby B., and Richard R. Bootizin. "Near-Death Experiences and the Temporal Lobe." *Psychological Science: A Journal of the American Psychological Society.* 15.4 (2004): 254-258.
[20] Ibid., p. 257.
[21] Greyson, C. Bruce. As quoted by Anahad O'Connor. "Following a Bright Light to a Calmer Tomorrow." *The New York Times.* 13 April 2004.
[22] Cranston, Sylvia, and Carey Williams. *Reincarnation: A New Horizon in Science, Religion, and Society.* Pasadena: Theosophical University Press, 1993, p. 68.
[23] Ibid., pp. 66-68.
[24] Kastenbaum, Robert J., Ph.D. *Death, Society, and Human Experience.* 8th Ed. Boston: Allyn & Bacon, 2003.
[25] There is also an American Society of Psychical Research founded in 1885, three years after the British one, and which was a branch of it briefly. Both were guided by William James, among others, and both thrive today.
[26] A preliminary study by NDE researcher and author Dr. Kenneth Ring shows a relationship between an abusive childhood, the ability to alter one's level of consciousness (which he suggests can be a defensive

escape mechanism) and the ability to have and recall a Near-Death Experience.
27 Armstrong, Karen. Conversation. Westar Institute Spring Conference. New York. 4-6 March 2004.
28 Harris Poll. "Most Americans Believe in Ghosts: Survey Shows 1/3 Accept Astrology, 1/4 Reincarnation." *World Net Daily.* Grants Pass, OR. 27 February 2003. <http://www.worldnetdaily.com>

Chapter 11

All Things Considered

> *I'm not an atheist, and I don't think I can call myself a pantheist. We are in a position of a little child entering a huge library filled with books in many languages. The child knows someone must have written those books. It does not know how. It does not understand the languages in which they're written. The child dimly suspects a mysterious order in the arrangement of the books but doesn't know what it is. That, it seems to me, is the attitude of even the most intelligent human being toward God.*
> —Albert Einstein

The challenges and horizons set out in Part III will have done their job if they converge in a direction of relief and resolution for those in the broad middle between committed atheists and staunch afterlife believers. Studies cited have revealed that these uncertain many are more prone to heightened fears of dying.

Previous chapters have addressed this relationship between degrees of religious belief and lessened death anxiety, as well as the fears of unmet potentials and extinction with insignificance. The need to make something of oneself, seen in the call to individuated success that underscores America's marked Western individualism, has been shown in its adversarial role to these death fears. A consensus of secular death educators is the relief provided by commitments, whether religious or not, which supercede and move away from the ego.

Additional attention has been given to the uniquely resilient strength of optimistic American afterlife belief among Western countries and the positive historical turnaround in the 20th century among the medical community affecting all aspects of the terminal stage itself. As noted, as the millenium began, both brought this country generally improved circumstances for dying.

But then, so much changed on September 11, 2001. The future is not what it used to be. It must be navigated without rutters.

At the end of the PBS *Power of Myth* series, Bill Moyers asked Joseph Campbell what the mythology to come would look like. Campbell responded that the new myth would be global, involving all peoples. An appropriate symbol would be that image of Earth, he said, as seen from the spacecraft, with continents and oceans misting together.

So the myth is turning out to be.

If Joseph Campbell were still alive, how would he interpret the new global warriors? Where in the forest would he see any pure knights? Will the myth be an Armageddon journey where, far from the burnt metal of all the armor, green sprigs of new growth appear and the air is filled with an unknown language?

If Campbell were still alive, I would wish for a wise producer to bring together Campbell and Karen Armstrong in conversation. Their worlds of historical mythology and theology have reflected each other since religion and art defined the cave dwellers' attempt to give meaning to their existence. I can think of no better minds to thrash around where contemporary mythic themes and religious struggles are united in warning about the future. I suspect death anxiety, in the guise of disillusionment and uncertainty, would play a new and very prominent role.

The British and European disillusionment and disbelief in

a loving and just God have not lessened and only increased the thirst for spiritual experience in those countries. Whether ongoing terrorism and mass death will similarly erode a belief in God—and by extension an afterlife—in this country is unknown. What is known is that non-theistic philosophies, such as Buddhism and New Age, and interior enlightenment with or without the help of a therapist are thriving ways of life. Spirituality has surpassed religion as a publishing house category. Yoga is "hot" everywhere, as is meditation. Both are Eastern trails to mysticism.

The clamor for psychic phenomena and its stars is deafening. Within a generation the jump in poll numbers of those who accept ghosts and reincarnation is a phenomenon in itself. Ghosts and reincarnation both proclaim the same word—afterlife! Whether God or a ticket back, just make sure it has a green light.

I have a friend who is a devout, old-line Episcopalian and an avid fan of the pet psychic show. A smorgasbord of supernatural beliefs, including Christian and occult, fit together compatibly these days in a growing number of shopping baskets. However, spirituality and a spiritual life are not defined by these.

Spirituality and Faith

Another among my friends is an atheist whose Ph.D. mental credentials hit a wall when confronted with "spiritual" and "Buddhism." All the same mumbo-jumbo to him. It would take Madelyn Murray O'Hare to convince him that both are ways of traveling in this life, irrespective of supernatural beliefs.

I hope he is in the minority because the concepts of spirituality and faith form the linchpin between theists, non-theists and atheists as well as being the common denominator in the vocabularies of religions and secular death education. It is a good sign that "spirituality" is as much of a stumbling block as "God" when the question of definition is raised. Dame Cicely Saunders, founder of the Hospice movement, gave a secular point of departure by expansively defining spiritual as "the whole area of thought concerning moral values throughout life." She further describes the root of spiritual pain as the despairing feeling of meaninglessness as well as of unfinished business.[1]

Separately, there is the *spirituality of personal sacred spaces* that we find or create both without and within. Then, there is Martin Buber who might have seen these joined in an "I—thou" relationship of communion and mutuality when the other person is not an object of use. My own best stab at defining spirituality is as a dimension both inside myself and outside all around. Those moments when those two planes of existence—one immanent, one transcending, resonate together are as close to the kingdom as it gets.

How is this word understood by others? Besides religion, art is another manifestation and interpretation of spirituality, or the sacred. Robert Wuthnow, Professor of Sociology at Princeton, interviewed a wide variety of performing, visual and literary artists. He sought their intuition of the nature of spirituality as expressed symbolically in their work.

Among their attempts to describe "The Divine Mystery" are the phrases "inner sense of the supernatural" and "a direct experiential connection with God." Where one experiences spirituality in an ocean breeze on her face and intuits God as a guiding spirit, another finds an "indirect sense of transcendence through her connections with other people" even more than in and with nature. One who had trouble defining "spirituality" is nonetheless convinced that "there is some spiritual force that unifies everything." Getting in touch with that unity and "living more in tune with it" is this person's goal.[2]

Of these artists, dancer Jamel Gaines distinguishes between religion and spirituality yet feels a link between the two is valuable. Throughout childhood he attended an all-Black Baptist Church. In college, on the road with the Jubilation Dance Company, his direction moved from God and Jesus talk to talk of spirituality. Other company members spoke of the Creator as opposed to God or Jesus, "and their idea of spirituality focused on the energy or spirit that might be evident in dance itself." Gaines' spirituality is in every particle; moreover, it is greater than the particle, and formal religion is a way to "focus the diffuse power inherent in spirituality." He feels some divine energy at times fills him when he dances.

Another, Jon Davis, cannot relate to a divine being or transcendence in relationships yet ascribes to the presence of some form of universal but hidden Truth or Reality, of which only glimpses can be had. He believes in epiphanies that he experiences in nature and in writing. Wuthnow says, "If the spiritual dimension is ultimately a mystery, these artists nevertheless insist that it can be experienced partially and momentarily."[3]

Glimpsing this *mystery*, partially and momentarily, is the path of mysticism. Egoless and in a ecstatic state of detachment, mystics seek direct, unmediated experience of the divine within themselves, intuiting the sacred as both immanent and omnipresent. This reflects both Eastern non-theistic spirituality as well as Jesus' reported words in the Gnostic Gospel of Thomas, "Split wood. I am there."

As noted earlier, the goal of Sufism, the mystical arm of Islam is to achieve an experience of the divine, at which point all religious distinctions of Jew, Christian, Muslim fall away and become meaningless. The Sufi ecstatic becomes all of them and none of them, for the only relevance is the direct experience.

In the 18th century among notable mystics in Judaism was a poor, Polish faith healer, Baal Shem Tov, known as The Besht. Founder of the sect of Hasidism, he reinterpreted positively the disastrous explosion and splintering to Earth of divine sparks, derived from an early form of Kabbalism. He believed there exist holy sparks of God's glory in *all* things of the world, in our actions and even our sins. It was each Hasid's responsibility to search within as well as without to recognize and unite with the divine spark, to be redeemed and to redeem one's personal world. The Besht incorporated music, song, joy and also intensely concentrated meditation to raise the sparks.

Among Christian mystics, Meister Eckhart of the 14th century is popular. "To be is God" and "Those who believe that God is something outside themselves know not the truth" are famous quotes. I never think of Eckhart without recalling another quote which a religion professor gave in an attempt to capture this mystic's rapturous delivery: "The day I was born the heavens opened and the angels sang, 'Here's God!'" he repeated, with the full force and flavor of Ed McMahon's old *Tonight Show* introduction, "Here's Johnny!"[4]

These mystics were all tied to monotheistic religions.

To Albert Einstein and many others, the spiritual emotion of the mystical has nothing to do with religion: "The spiritual geniuses of all ages had no use for dogma, doctrine, creeds, churches, as well as no God conceived in man's image, all based on archaic superstition. My faith has always been in intuition, grounded in mysticism. I believe in Mystery. *The most profound spiritual emotion that we can experience is the sensation of the mystical;* to stand before the Mystery in awe and wonder is at the heart of all true art and science." To Nobel Prize-winning physicist and atheist Stephen Weinberg, religious superstition damages human dignity and growth.

Then there is William Edelen's overview: "Practically all Nobel Physicists have said their most perceptive insights came through mystical intuition. Mysticism has nothing to do with organized religion. In fact, it is the antithesis of 'religion'."[5] I suppose he means antithesis in freedom of spirit and thought when and where they are fettered by the constraint of belief.

A molecular biologist, Ursula Goodenough, wrote that her scientist's understanding of the cosmos left her with a despairing sense of nihilism. Finally, she found a way to "deflect the apparent pointlessness of it all by realizing that I don't have to seek a point. In any of it. Instead, I can see it as the locus of Mystery. The Mystery of why there is anything at all, rather than nothing. The Mystery of where the laws of physics came from. The Mystery of why the universe seems so strange." Goodenough rejects the word "God" which is often the title given this mystery since it connotes a creator figure. More profoundly, she says, "Deism spoils my covenant with Mystery. To assign attributes to Mystery is to disenchant it, to take away its luminance."[6]

What she describes can be a comforting meeting ground and resolution for many people. Hers is a spiritual emotion, through which the Mystery and mystical intuition make themselves known. When she first lay back under a night sky and contemplated the universe from a scientist's perspective, she wept for her adolescent loss—the realization that she didn't need to have answers or even seek answers to the Big Questions was an epiphany for her. Then, looking up at the unseen galaxies, she experienced their enormity and the wonder and awe of the cosmic and quantum Mystery.

On my part, I imagined myself similarly staring into the stars and blackness. Moreover, I imagined myself quietly dying there on the ground, just so. The feeling of absolute peace and warmth came strongly through me as I released myself into the dark. It was sublime. I would never have expected that the childhood Protector could be so easily and beautifully replaced.

The Buddha was full of jewels to help us on the journey. One of them addresses the knots of big questions, to which Goodenough referred, that strangle our spiritual growth if we seek miserably for answers. He tells the story of the man who is struck by an arrow which pierces his lung. Agitated, he wants to know who has done this dreadful thing and what his motive was. Meanwhile, he is getting closer and closer to death. "Pull out the arrow," advises Buddha. "You may never have answers, and your life will be over."

The Buddha brings to mind the spiritual practice of meditation. Hindu and Buddhist yogi understand well the spiritual function of breath in quieting the mind to a point of clarity in its approach to Brahman or to Nirvana. Emptying the cluttered mind and focusing on the still point within is a path of spirituality many walk. Unfortunately, I am a failure at that. It is the only time my mind wants to do a grocery list.

Determined to come clear, I went to a Buddhist Institute in Berkeley, California, for a meditation weekend surrounded by candles and golden buddhas. For two hours the first night, I was told to imagine a gently flaming white lotus in my throat. Not a chance. Boredom, back pain and the choice of coffees at the nearby coffeehouse filled my every pore. I respectfully raised my hand. "I'm having trouble with the lotus. May I substitute a gardenia?" No one giggled; I was sincere, after all. "Yes, you may."

Perhaps I figured if I visualized my beloved gardenia down my throat, I could open my mouth and smell it, thereby improving my mood and Nirvana chances. In short, except for the coffeehouse, I have blocked out the memory of the rest of the weekend.

Often, what is authentic to one's self is right there all along and is not recognized for what it is. Joseph Campbell was asked what he did to meditate. His answer was two words, and they speak for both of us. "I underline," he replied. Appropriately, the most profound spiritual meditation I have had, punctuated with several moments of transcendence, was reading *A Joseph Campbell Companion: Reflections on the Art of Living* edited by Diane Osbon. When I read such a book, pen in hand, people have to yell in my face to break through the *personal sacred space*.

A great *faith*-based, not religion-based, force has been giving meaning to lives for decades now. The Twelve-Step Program is a spiritual process, one which involves reliance on a transcending power beyond Self. However, doctrinal religion may be individually added or absent.

The dictionary definition of a significant relationship or behavioral pattern in a group or community fits the spiritual foundation of Twelve-Step Programs. Probably the most profound and accessible death-and-rebirth experience our culture offers to those in need, the Program has transformed lives and brought self-esteem to them.

Besides to addictive or behavioral problems, it seems it could be logically applied to an unmanageable fear or imminent threat of death with its many cathartic elements, including that of trust and release. Besides the admission of lack of control, the only other requirements are faith in a healing power greater and outside the self and a person with whom to work the Steps.

The Program provides the chief defenses against the fears of death. It brings meaning to a life by requiring a commitment which neatly fulfills the parameters expressed by Kavanaugh. Equally significant, it also ensures ongoing self-esteem and a structure for it. For these reasons, it is my conviction that an alcoholic or other addict who has been working the Steps will not have the death anxiety one might suppose. Although I have not seen polls or research to support this, I believe the guilt of wasted years and shameful acts is more than offset by the transforming nature of this purifying renewal process and the feelings of enormous self-respect it brings.

Following are some relatives of spiritual humanism, which historically has stressed creativity and contributions to one's fellow beings. Humanism, rooted in 18th-century religious skepticism, was preceded by Epicureanism. In a time of rampant, superstitious fears of death, Epicurus (342-270 B.C.) taught that desire for immortality was a source of anxiety and thus destructive, impeding value and enjoyment of this life.

Three centuries before Jesus, the common Epicurean epitaph read, "I was not, I am not, I do not mind." Epicurus wrote a friend from his deathbed, "On this truly happy day of my life, as I am at the point of death, I write this to you....against all this [disease] is the joy in my heart at the recollection of my conversation with you." Humanism's essence throughout history lies in the fulfillment of one's potentials and in helping others.[7] There is that duo again—"completeness" and compassion.

Don Cupitt preaches the *spirituality of outwardness* instead of the spirituality of mystical inwardness. There are three themes to his spiritual concept. One aspect already mentioned is "Solar Living," the constant outpouring and burning out of one's energies, like the sun. "We can get ourselves together only by leaving ourselves behind—to live by dying all the time" in symbolic self-expression.

Second is recognition of the "Blissful Void, the abstract sacred, the cool sublime, and the disappearance of the self into immanence, objectivity and nothingness." He draws an analogy between the blissful void and the goal of most meditation and contemplative prayer.

The third element is "the Eye of God." This simply means, even if you are an atheist, looking at both yourself and your world as though through the eyes of God. This enhances consciousness, provides a conscience and brings greater clarity of moral vision. Wonderfully, he adds, "It also opens great humorous possibilities, which Jews and East Europeans have exploited very effectively. The God's-eye vision is also the comic vision."[8]

A handy pair of glasses, God's Eye must see all the clinging climbers as a comic case in point.

An article about Cupitt quoted him thus: "Quickly we must die to death, escape from the tyranny of this natural ego that clings so hopelessly to life, and enter upon a new life and divine form of consciousness, disinterested, universal, non-egoistic and free." However, it is a line of the article's author, Trevor Greenfield, which captured my attention. "*We must strive to attain a spiritual consciousness because in doing so we lose the old ego, the part of us which fears death.*" [9]

Greenfield makes the point here which I have hammered, that it is the ego only which fears death. (This is the same street definition of ego we use when we say, "Damn, she has a big ego!") But there is far more meat in his sentence. Specifically, it is in the striving for and attaining of an everyday, spiritual consciousness that the ego is lost. This chapter gives names to a few of the ways of seeing (perspectives again) that spiritual consciousness can take.

Another sun-involved spirituality harks back to earlier words written. The *spirituality of Gaia*, our planetary life-support system, is founded on reverence for Gaia's gifts and responsibility for this space and this moment instead of for another space and future moments beyond Earth. Gaia spirituality "means to live *as if* earth is what in fact it is: the ground of my being. *As if* everything I am and everything I have is, ultimately, what it is: Earth's gift to me. *As if* my self-regulation is intimately connected, in all its aspects, with the self-regulation of Gaia; with her ability to maintain optimal conditions for the physiological processes which sustain all life. Which is indeed the case." [10]

Walks out in nature of the bird-listening-and-identifying groups for the blind come to mind as profound experiences of Gaia spirituality and her covenant with us. Hindus bond the natural world with *Shakti*, divine energy or power moving through all. A prime example is the River Ganges which Hindus call "Mother" and believe to be "a liquid form of

Shakti." [11] Native American prayers draw its pictures. This covenant is felt everywhere.

Then, there is what I call the *spirituality of the offering*. The man who tied the desire for immortality to the cause of human evil, Ernest Becker, also wrote, "The most any one of us can seem to do is to fashion something—an object or ourselves—and drop it into the confusion, make an offering of it, so to speak, to the life force."[12] For families, the nurturing of children can be a phenomenal sacred offering, one that is consciously fashioned. As Carl Jung imagined, his deeds would stand at the grave with him, as part of the offering there to turn over to the unknown. Whether the life force, the Mystery or a traditional Being fills the transcendent space to which the offering is made, the commitment to it will bring all one needs to face death without anxiety.

To those like me who refuse to give up on the Mystery—by whatever name—there is the wisdom of hope in these instructions on dying which Jeremy Taylor gave in his 1651 bestseller *The Rule and Exercises of Holy Dying*, with which I began this text. With whatever concept the offering's creator substitutes for "God," Taylor's admonition makes a striking point about a fixation on the appeal of this life. He hands these hopeful words to the person who is afraid of death with a "transporting fear...either loves this world too much, or dares not trust God for the next." Intrinsic to the spirituality of the offering one makes is the trusting act and peace of *letting go*.

I see another release imperative, ideally practiced through mid-life. It is the Release of Judgment, both of others and that which others have of us. The latter is especially hard to slough off because deeply embedded anger and negative self-image are stealth attachments to it. I turn to this exercise to release my projections onto others, which helps also to release myself from their own toward me. I visualize each problem person in an earlier, pre-programmed time, and there I let go of anger and judgment. Some searches have challenged my imagination, but that place in their history *and my own* does exist before the conditioning of circumstances or culture became divisive. This practice of release brings a spiritual transformation and opens wide the door into Big Mind. *The spirituality of empathy*, found on this path of letting go of judgment, is my final example.

Campbell notes that, in the Parzival Legend, the Grail represents the highest *spiritual* fulfillment. The lesson for the Middle Ages was that supernatural grace gained through the church's judgment killed natural grace, "the energy of nature" whose natural tendency is to the spirit. It could only be cured "by the spontaneous act of a noble heart, whose impulse is not of the *ego*, but of love—and love in the sense not of sexual love, but of *compassion*. That's the Grail problem."[13]

The reasons Christian Crusaders slaughtered tens of thousands of Muslims and Jews in Jerusalem go way back. Centuries of persecution complexes, Jewish pogroms and misconceptions about Muhammad followed. The Grail, lost through the ego of exclusive knighthood identities, can only be regained through unconditional compassion—empathy and identity *with* the other. Karen Armstrong notes that compassion and social justice are historically visible, particularly in both Judaism and Islam, that all religions historically have proclaimed the need to "edit the ego" and move beyond it.

Armstrong calls for the *spirituality of empathy*. She has found the practice of compassion leads "directly to a divine encounter....[It] is a habit of the mind that is transforming...and has changed the way I experience the world. *Compassion* has been advocated by all the great faiths because it has been found to be the safest and surest means of attaining enlightenment. It *dethrones the ego* from the center of our lives and puts *others* there, breaking down the carapace of selfishness that holds us back from *an experience of the sacred.*"[14]

I read these magnificent lines after I had completed Part I and was delighted to see how perfectly their religious orientation expresses the secular insights in the first chapters. I had known, from the beginning, that if I never mentioned one religious figure or doctrine by way of example and only cited Kastenbaum, Shneidman, Kavanaugh, Kalish, Feifel, Gorer, Aries, Goodman, Kearl, Lifton, McCarthy and so on, this still would be a *spiritual* book. It is the ego alone that fears death, the ego alone that stands in the way of experiencing the eternal.

Faith is more at home aligned with spirituality than inextricably tied to institutional, doctrinal religion. Armstrong credits the theologian Cantwell Smith with the clarification that it was recent Western error, spawned in the 18th century, that equated faith with acceptance of our man-made concept of God. Rather, faith was actually "the cultivation of a conviction that life had some ultimate meaning and value," despite contrarian evidence, as exemplified in great art.[15] *Faith is a belief in a final meaning and value to the journey—it may be just that simple and that powerful.*

The individual's ego in our culture is a tough nut to crack completely. However, the practices of faith thus defined and of the perspective of Big Mind are solid bets to create that opening in the frame. It was this same meaning of faith that Kavanaugh described in what I found to be the consensus of Western death educators for moving outside the ego and dispelling its fears of death. There are no better words to revisit in conclusion:

> *Faith is simply that total commitment of the entire person to an ideal, a way of life, a set of values, to anything or anyone beyond the narrow limitations of myself. God, mankind, the poor, science, human relations, growth and development, anything capable of bringing meaning and purpose to life....Near*

death, true belief in what you sincerely hold will bring peace and any promise you need for your future.

---

[1] Saunders, Cicely. "Spiritual Pain." *Hospital Chaplain.* St. Christopher's Fourth International Conference. March 1988.

[2] Wuthnow, Robert. *Creative Spirituality: The Way of the Artist.* Berkeley, Los Angeles, London: University of California Press, 2001, pp. 23-25.

[3] Ibid., pp. 25-28.

[4] Laughlin, Paul Allen. Symposium. "Comparative Religions." Westar Institute. Santa Rosa, CA. October 2002.

[5] Edelen, William. "Two Worthy Heroes: Men of Science, Passion, Mysticism." *Santa Barbara News-Press.* 5 January 2003. G3.

[6] Goodenough, Ursula. *Sacred Depths of Nature.* New York & Oxford: Oxford University Press, 2000, pp. 10-13.

[7] Gatliffe, Eleanor D. *Death in the Classroom: A Resource Book for Teachers and Others.* London: Epworth, 1988.

[8] Cupitt, Don. *After God: The Future of Religion.* New York: Basic Books, 1997, pp. 84-90.

[9] Greenfield, Trevor. "A Brief History of Radical Theology: Part 9—Cupitt, Taking Leave of God." *Sea of Faith.* Loughborough, UK: Sea of Faith Network. 64. March 2004. (emphasis mine)

[10] Primavesi, Anne. *Gaia's Gift: Earth, Ourselves, and God After Copernicus.* London & New York: Routledge: 2003, p. 85.

[11] Eck, Diane. *Encountering God.* Boston: Beacon Press, 1993, p. 139.

[12] Becker, Ernest. *The Denial of Death.* New York: Free Press, 1973, p. 285.

[13] Campbell, Joseph. "In Search of the Holy Grail: The Parzival Legend." *Transformations of Myth Through Time.* New York: Harper & Row, 1990, pp. 254-55. (emphasis mine)

[14] Armstrong, Karen. *The Spiral Staircase: My Climb out of Darkness.* New York & Toronto: Knopf, 2004, p. 296.

[15] Ibid., p. 292.

*Identity, commitment and direction
are the basic channels
of personal human meaning.*
—**Imara**

AFTERWORDS

*Ideals are like stars:
you will not succeed in touching them with your hands, but,
like the sea-faring man on the desert of water, you choose them
as your guides, and following them,
you reach your destiny.*
—**Carl Schurz**

*The world is not interested in
the storms you encountered, but
did you bring in the ship?*
—**William McFee**

No wind serves him who has no destined port.
—**Michel de Montaigne**

Two Women and a Boat

"Seductive" was the adjective I used to describe living in that billionaired section of Santa Barbara called Montecito. As in mindless, rootless, stressless *Southern California.* There, it seemed, women in divorce went to José Eber instead of to pieces. In truth, one I knew got a real lift out of her divorce. Her ex-husband was a plastic surgeon, and he gave her bigger breasts as a parting gift. *Very S.C.* And I loved and needed Southern California's seduction. For awhile.

"Seduce," however, means to lead astray or draw away, as from principles or rectitude, to beguile or entice. I needed to believe the enchanted, surreal life there indeed led one off course, so that I could muster the will to leave.

Walking its beach one day, I devised a metaphor that said all that and more. Really friendly people are bobbing around in little boats, having a picnic. It is a true Pissaro-Renoir visual, complete with top hats tipping and parasols twirling in the sun. No one leaves, for departure would require a separate boat and aloneness. Everyone waves daintily at all the other bobbing boats and parasols, unaware of the problem.

You see, they have no anchors or ports to hold their vision. They have no anchoring commitments to ground them or stow aboard when they journeyed, to be put down again in new places and stages along the way. And they have fashioned no ports at all towards which to sail.

This metaphor stayed with me long after I moved. It has taken on a creative life of its own and become a shorthand image that I can pull up when I am drifting. The challenge is to fill the boat with the *rutters* I know well and can rely on to guide me successfully into the port of my making. And to inner peace in my final days.

Anyone can have such a boat. It is as free and seaworthy as one's imagination! The spiritual *rutters* can include books, a parent, a mentor or a role model. One might be a deceased historical personage of whom a plethora of biographies have clearly illuminated his or her personality and views. (I recall what a bum rap Hillary Clinton received for imagining the advice she would get from Eleanor Roosevelt. From the media portrayal of the consultation, you would think Clinton poured Roosevelt a Coke® and complimented her on her hat!)

This is not an escapist fantasy. It is a compact, evocative image whose components represent meaningful direction and goals, commitments and the likely reactions of trusted, revered role models to a personal crisis or pending decision. The rutters will change over time and alter slightly the port and course. I may never reach my port, but I always will have it in sight. Book companions I have chosen for the current lap of the journey are *A Joseph Campbell Companion* and a book of the Buddha's insights, since he spoke directly to my shortcomings.

Defensively, though, I admit that the Buddha had an unfortunate blind spot. It is one typical of those other prophets of the Axial, or Pivotal, Age who encouraged questioning everything and accepting nothing as certain, and no one as authority but oneself, and the truth came from within. To their credit, in courage they denounced animal sacrifice and such barbaric vestiges. They exhorted the ethic of the Golden Rule, non-orthodox inner revelation and practical compassion as replacement for the ego. The focus was on this life, not another supernatural one.[1] Unfortunately, these sages, reflecting their times, also were mostly male chauvinists.

If it helps you on your journey to believe in a Supreme Being, an afterlife, nihilism or Buddhist philosophy, then do. If it doesn't, don't. But do not waste a precious lifetime seeking big, elusive answers. Awake to this moment, drop your ego needs and practice compassion with others in order to experience happiness and moments of transcendence. I love the Buddha for his lessons in perspective and letting go. A good dose of Buddha would have cured that poor climber hanging off the cliff, clinging desperately to his ego.

For coping: a role model for morale

In spirit, I have chosen two women as inspiring company—for this stage of the journey anyway. One of these human *rutters,* my role model for morale, is my fantasy pal, Sarah Bernhardt.

You may never bring in the ship, and it doesn't matter.

Of all the responses I intuited she would give, none contained more truth or liberation or effected more change, apart from my research. How Buddha it sounds, too. It is a one-line weapon against my old fear of incompleteness. She vanquished storms and flamboyantly sailed to port. Hers was an indomitable hand, having to bring her own ship back on course time and again. Ultimately, Sarah brought in her ship.

Of course, it could be said that Sarah is really only bits of my authentic self still surfacing, part of which had felt worn down and buried and part of which had never been called forth to bloom. I see no reason to probe the genesis as long as thoughts of her imagined responses bring such salutary joy and, often, better perspective. In truth, I rarely think of her more than semi-annually at most. However, for this point in my life, I am smart enough to recognize the perfect spiritual first mate *for morale.* As such, I hope to make her wisdom, humor and laughter more prominent in my coping strategy.

For perspective and meaning: another role model
The second human *rutter* I have put, *in spirit*, in my boat is one who is quite alive today. I had read a number of Karen Armstrong's books previously as background.

It was not until I had completed secular conclusions for Part I, about ego and compassionate empathy with others, that I read *The Spiral Staircase*. In this autobiography, she deduces the same common denominators in world religions as I had in secular death education. Because she is such a stellar example of the hero's journey to an authentic life, I went back and parted paragraphs to include her personal story.

More significantly, though, has been her meaning for me personally. I learned we share the same Wordsworth mantra, finding "strength in what remains behind" after loss. We have identical religious views and current world concerns. I understand what she means by moments of transcendence in her reading (for me, in reading and in nature) and agree there is no need to give these brief glimpses a name.

There was a lonely, vulnerable, *needy*, period in her life that she protected behind an intellectual barrier of words and caustic wit. An injured, frightened animal lashing out she further pictured. In that full description, although the causes were so different, she used the same words I had for and to myself many times. Our passions and causes are apparently the same; emotions we have truly suffered are also, even though we came to them from different directions.

Armstrong has inspired my respect and gratitude for setting the standard of achievement both in her professional study of theology and in her personal climb from darkness. If my boat had reality in this world, and if I could have one last daydream come true, it would be to heal today's world.

My fantasy is to have Jesus and Muhammad return as boatmates and hold what would surely be the Ultimate Press Conference. Karen Armstrong would contribute questions and transcribe their answers. I believe that these enlightened, courageous giants would answer with one voice. Nor do I doubt for a second that they would have profound respect and understanding for one another, as indeed Muhammad did for Jesus, who preceded him in death, and for Judaism particularly.

I would like to know this inspired and inspiring prophet better, and, in reality, am reading biographies of him currently. As Armstrong points out in *Muhammad*, the Qur'an is considered among the most, if not *the* most, magnificent poetic expression of Arabic language ever written, religious or otherwise, moving readers and listeners to tears.

The historical Jesus would represent his Jewish brethren also, since he was first, last and always a Jew. I am totally enamored of the Jesus I have come to know, one whose revolutionary message "Love thy enemies" has always been too hard, except perhaps for the Quakers and Buddhists as groups, to embrace. Many of his followers choose instead to love only their neighbors, which is no stretch in most neighborhoods.

I would never dream of putting words into Armstrong's mouth, so here are her own words, re-used to pose questions for these two gifted teachers.

"I discovered that in all three of the religions of Abraham [Judaism, Islam, Christianity], fundamentalist movements distort the traditions they are trying to defend by emphasizing the belligerent elements in their tradition and overlooking the insistent and crucial demand for compassion."[2]

Discuss and resolve. The world badly needs clarification.

"Our task now is to mend our broken world; if religion cannot do that, it is worthless."[3]

Comment.

I wish also for the following questions to again be put to Armstrong, just as they were in a *New York Times* interview. Asked why there have been so many wars if world religions have such great similarities among them, she responded that the culprit was egotism, since compassion has never really been in vogue and many are using their God as an approving green light for "some of their worst fantasies about other people."

About any hope for the future of religion, she commented that we need to weed out the "egotistical and lazy theology" which has accumulated over time, that which has led to the belief that "my God is better than your God." She pointed out that Jung had warned that a lot of religion keeps us from any religious experience. Armstrong was asked if she believes in an afterlife. "I am not interested in the afterlife. *Religion is supposed to be about losing your ego, not preserving it* eternally in optimum conditions."[4]

Refocusing to a compassionate identity with *others* in *this* world does not negate a personal covenant with God, the Mystery, moments of transcendence, ethical philosophies or an individual port for aspirations. In fact, this ego loss is the *only* path to *any* of these! According to all secular educators and theology, it also is the surest path to overcoming the fears of death. My research, all and always, ends up right there. With a change of perspective.

---

[1] These points about the sages of the Axial Age are a favorite theme of Karen Armstrong in her presentations.

[2] Armstrong, Karen. *The Spiral Staircase: My Climb out of Darkness*. New York & Toronto: Knopf, 2004, p. 295.

[3] Ibid., p. 304. Armstrong then adds that what the world needs rather than religious certainty and belief is "compassionate action and practically expressed respect for the sacred value of all human beings—even our enemies." Interviewed by Michael Valpy ("God is Big These Days." *Shambhala Sun*. January 2005, pp. 38-41), Armstrong states that after Auschwitz and September 11, "the only thing that will save our world" is a fresh spiritual quest based on a realistic comprehension of current world religion. Where will it lead? "I don't believe it will be a belief in a conventional god, but that's of no interest or importance."

[4] Solomon, Deborah. "Taking Religious Liberties." *The New York Times*. 6:17. 4 April 2004. (emphasis mine)

BIBLIOGRAPHY

Addison, Joseph. *Cato: A Tragedy in Five Acts.* 1713.
American Heritage Dictionary, The.
Aries, Philip. *Centuries of Childhood.* New York: Knopf, 1962.
—. *Western Attitudes Toward Death: From the Middle Ages to the Present.* Baltimore & London: John Hopkins University Press, 1974.
Armstrong, Karen. Conversation. Westar Institute Spring Conference. New York, 4-6 March 2004.
—. *A History of God: The 4000-Year Quest of Judaism, Christianity and Islam.* New York: Knopf, 1994.
—. *Islam: A Short History.* New York: Modern Library, 2000.
—. *Muhammad: A Biography of the Prophet.* San Francisco: HarperCollins, 1993.
—. Presentations. "Some Tips from the Axial Age" and "The Spiral Staircase." Westar Institute Spring Conference. New York, 4-6 March 2004.
—. *The Spiral Staircase: My Climb out of Darkness.* New York & Toronto: Knopf, 2004.
Atchley, Robert C. *Social Forces of Aging.* Belmont, CA: Wadsworth Thomson Learning, 2000.
Bardis, Panos. *History of Thanotology.* Washington, D.C.: University Press of America, 1981.
Barrett, Deirdre. "Dreams of Death." *Omega: Journal of Death and Dying.* Robert J. Kastenbaum, Ph.D., ed. Farmingdale, NY: Baywood. 19.1 (1988-89).
Barry, Susan. "Alcoholics and Death Anxiety." *The Forum: A Publication of the Association for Death Education and Counseling.* West Hartford, CT: Lebon Press Inc. 17.2 (1992).
Baumeister, Roy F. *Meanings in Life.* New York: The Guilford Press, 1991.
Becker, Ernest, Dr. *The Denial of Death.* New York: Free Press, 1973.
—. *Escape from Evil.* New York: Free Press, 1973.
Bernhardt, Sarah. *My Double Life: The Memoirs of Sarah Bernhardt.* Albany: State University of New York Press, 1999.
Boston, Sarah, and Rachel Trezise. *Merely Mortal: Coping with Dying, Death and Bereavement.* London: Methuen, in association with Channel Four Television Co., Ltd., 1987.
Boyle, Joan M., and James E. Morriss. *The Mirror of Time: Images of Aging and Dying.* New York: Greenwood, 1987.

Bremmer, Jan N. *The Rise and Fall of the Afterlife.* New York: Routledge, 2002.
Britton, Willoughby B., and Richard R. Bootzin. "Near-Death Experiences and the Temporal Lobe." *Psychological Science: A Journal of the American Psychological Society.* Ithaca, NY: Blackwell. 15.4 (2004).
Brokenleg, Martin, and David Middleton. "Native Americans: Adapting, Yet Retaining." *Ethnic Variations in Dying, Death, and Grief: Diversity in Universality.* Donald P. Irish, Kathleen F. Lundquist and Vivian Jenkins Nelson, eds. Washington, D.C.: Taylor & Francis, 1993.
Brown, Melanie. *Attaining Personal Greatness: One Book for Life.* New York: Morrow, 1987.
Buckman, Dr. Robert. *I Don't Know What to Say: How to Help and Support Someone Who is Dying.* London: Papermac, 1988.
Budge, Sir E.A. Wallis. *The Book of the Dead: With a New Introduction by David Lorimer.* London: Arkana, 1985.
—. *Egyptian Religion: Egyptian Ideas of the Future Life.* London: Arkana, 1987.
Butler, Robert N., M.D. *Why Survive? Being Old in America.* New York: Harper & Row, 1975.
Byock, Ira, Dr. *Dying Well: The Prospect for Growth at the End of Life.* New York: Riverhead, 1997.
Campbell, Joseph. "In Search of the Holy Grail: The Parzival Legend." *Transformations of Myth Through Time.* New York: Harper & Row, 1990.
—. *Myths to Live By.* New York: Viking, 1972.
—. With Bill Moyers. *The Power of Myth.* 3rd Ed. Betty Sue Flowers, ed. New York: Doubleday, 1988.
Charmaz, Kathy, Glennys Howarth and Allan Kellehear, eds. *The Unknown Country: Death in Australia, Britain and the USA.* New York: St. Martin's Press, 1997.
Chua, Amy. *World on Fire: How Expanding Free-Market Democracy Breeds Ethnic Hatred and Global Instability.* New York: Doubleday, 2003.
Cohen, Gene D., M.D., Ph.D. *The Creative Age: Awakening Human Potential in the Second Half of Life.* New York: Avon Books, 2000.
Cranston, Sylvia, and Carey Williams. *Reincarnation: A New Horizon in Science, Religion, and Society.* Pasadena: Theosophical University Press, 1993.
Cupitt, Don. *After God: The Future of Religion.* New York: Basic Books, 1997.
—. *Emptiness and Brightness.* Santa Rosa, CA: Polebridge Press, 2001.

BIBLIOGRAPHY

Dunne, John S. *The City of the Gods: A Study in Myth and Mortality.* New York: Macmillan, 1965.

Dychtwald, Ken, Ph.D., and Joe Flower. *Age Wave: The Challenges and Opportunities of an Aging America.* Los Angeles: Tarcher, 1989.

Eck, Diane L. *Encountering God: A Spiritual Journey from Bozeman to Benares.* Boston: Beacon Press, 1993.

Edelen, William. "Two Worthy Heroes: Men of Science, Passion, Mysticism." *Santa Barbara News-Press.* 5 January 2003.

Editorial. "News to Chew Over: Eat Better and Live Longer." *Austin [TX] American-Statesman.* 21 September 2003.

Elias, Norbert. *The Loneliness of the Dying.* Oxford: Basil Blackwell, 1985.

Feifel, Herman, ed. *The Meaning of Death.* New York: McGraw-Hill, 1959.

Fisher, Mary Pat, and Lee W. Bailey. *An Anthology of Living Religions.* Upper Saddle River, NJ: Prentice-Hall, 2000.

Forbes, Malcolm, with Jeff Block. *They Went That-a-Way.* New York: Simon & Schuster, 1988.

Frankl, Viktor E. *Man's Search for Meaning.* New York: Touchstone Ed. 1984.

Friedman, Alan. Presentation. "Death as a Cultural Phenomenon." Humanities Research Center, The University of Texas at Austin. 6 November 2003.

Gallup Organization. Poll, December 1994. Quoted in George Bishop, "What Americans Really Believe." *Free Inquiry.* Amherst. Summer (1999).

Gatliffe, Eleanor D. *Death in the Classroom: A Resource Book for Teachers and Others.* London: Epworth, 1988.

Gehlek, Rimpoche Nawang. *Good Life, Good Death: Tibetan Wisdom on Reincarnation.* New York: Riverhead/Penguin-Putnam, 2001.

Ghandi, Mahatma. "For the Well-being of the Nation." *The Message of Mahatma Gandhi.* U S Mohan Rao, ed. New Delhi: Ministry of Information and Broadcasting, 1968.

Gill, Derek. *Quest: The Life of Elisabeth Kubler-Ross.* New York: Harper & Row, 1980.

Gold, Arthur. *The Divine Sarah: A Life of Sarah Bernhardt.* New York: Knopf, 1991.

Goldberg, Ivan K., Austin H. Kutscher and Sidney Malitz, eds. *Pain, Anxiety, and Grief: Pharmacotherapeutic Care of the Dying Patient.* New York: Columbia University, 1986.

Gonda, Thomas Andrew, M.D., and John Edward Ruark, M.D. *Dying Dignified: The Health Professional's Guide to Care.* Menlo Park, CA: Addison-Wesley, 1984.

Goodenough, Ursula. *Sacred Depths of Nature.* New York & Oxford: Oxford University Press, 2000.

Goodman, Lisl Marburg, Dr. *Death and the Creative Life.* New York: Springer, 1981.

Gorer, Geoffrey. *Death, Grief, and Mourning.* New York: Doubleday, 1965.

Green, Betty R., and Donald P. Irish. *Death Education: Preparation for Living.* Cambridge: Schenkman, 1971.

Greenfield, Trevor. "A Brief History of Radical Theology: Part 9—Cupitt, Taking Leave of God." *Sea of Faith.* Loughborough, UK: Sea of Faith Network. March 2004.

Greyson, C. Bruce. "Following a Bright Light to a Calmer Tomorrow." As quoted by Anahad O'Connor. *The New York Times.* 13 April 2004.

Hagglund, Tor-jorn. *Dying: A Psychoanalytic Study with Special Reference to Individual Creativity and Defensive Organization.* New York: International Universities Press, 1978.

Harris, Jill. "Religious Ritual for a Secular Society." *Sea of Faith.* Loughborough, UK: Sea of Faith Network. January 2004.

Harris Poll. "Most Americans Believe in Ghosts: Survey Shows 1/3 Accept Astrology, 1/4 Reincarnation." *World Net Daily.* Grants Pass, OR. 27 February 2003. <http://www.worldnetdaily.com>

Hillenbrand Laura. *Seabiscuit: An American Legend.* New York: Random House, 2001. Illustrated Ed., 2003.

Holck, Frederick. "Life Revisited: Parallels in Death Experiences." *Omega: Journal of Death and Dying.* Robert J. Kastenbaum, Ph.D., ed. Farmingdale, NY: Baywood. 9.1 (1978-79).

Holmes, Oliver Wendell, Jr. *Holmes-Einstein Letters.* (1910). London: Macmillan, 1964.

Huxley, Aldous. *Doors of Perception.* New York: Harper & Row, 1963.

James, William. *Memories and Studies.* New York: Longmans/Green, 1911.

Jung, Carl G. *Memories, Dreams, Reflections.* Recorded and edited by Aniela Jaffe. London: Collins, 1963.

Kalish, Richard A. "Death Educator as Deacon." *Omega: Journal of Death and Dying.* Robert J. Kastenbaum, Ph.D., ed. Farmingdale, NY: Baywood. 11.1 (1980-81).

Kapleau, Philip, ed. *The Wheel of Death.* New York: Harper & Row, 1971.

Kastenbaum, Robert J., Ph.D. *Death, Society, and Human Experience.* 8th Ed. Boston: Allyn & Bacon, 2003.

—. *Is There Life After Death?* New York: Prentice Hall, 1984.

—. *Is There Life After Death? The Latest Evidence Analysed.* Rev. Ed. London: Prion, 1995.

—. *On Our Way: The Final Passage Through Life and Death.* Berkeley & Los Angeles: University of California Press, 2004.
—. *The Psychology of Death.* 3rd Ed. New York: Springer, 2000.
—. And Beatrice Kastenbaum, eds. *Encyclopedia of Death.* Phoenix: Oryx Press, 1989.
Kavanaugh, Robert E. *Facing Death.* Los Angeles: Nash, 1972.
Kearl, Michael C. *Endings: A Sociology of Death and Dying.* New York & Oxford: Oxford University Press, 1989.
Knott, J. Eugene, et al. *Thanatopics: Activities and Exercises for Confronting Death.* Lexington: Lexington, 1989.
Kolata, Gina. "Low-Calorie-Diet Study Takes Scientists Aback." *The New York Times.* 19 September 2003.
Krauss, Pesach. *Why Me? Coping with Grief, Loss and Change.* Morrie Goldfischer, ed. New York: Bantam, 1988.
Kubler-Ross, Elisabeth, Dr., ed. *Death: The Final Stage of Growth.* Englewood Cliffs, NJ: Prentice-Hall, 1975.
—. *On Death and Dying.* New York: Macmillan, 1969.
—. "Second Annual Louise Hart Memorial Lecture." Jansen Memorial Hospice. Bronxville, NY. 7 April 1987.
—. *Working It Through. Photographs by Mal Warshaw.* New York: Macmillan, 1982.
Labus, Janet G., and Faye H. Dambrot. "A Comparative Study of Terminally Ill Hospice and Hospital Patients." *Omega: Journal of Death and Dying.* Robert J. Kastenbaum, Ph.D., ed. Farmingdale, NY: Baywood. 16.3 (1985-86).
Laughlin, Paul Allen. Symposium. "Comparative Religions." Westar Institute. Santa Rosa, CA. October 2002.
Lee, Elizabeth, Dr. *In Your Own Time: A Guide for Patients and Their Carers Facing a Last Illness at Home.* 2nd Ed. New York: Oxford University Press, 2002.
Lee, Sander H. *Woody Allen's Angst: Philosophical Commentaries on His Serious Films.* Jefferson, NC, & London: McFarland & Co., Inc., 1997.
Lerner, Alan Jay. *The Street Where I Live.* (1978). Cambridge & New York: Da Capo Press, 1994.
Lieberman, E. James, M.D. *Acts of Will: The Life and Work of Otto Rank.* New York: Free Press, 1985.
Lifton, Robert Jay. *The Broken Connection: On Death and the Continuity of Life.* New York: Simon & Schuster, 1979.
— et al. *Six Lives, Six Deaths: Portraits from Modern Japan.* New Haven & London: Yale University Press, 1979.

Loehr, Davidson, Ph.D. Seminar. "Jesus: The Origins of Christianity and the Implications of 'Demythologizing' Western Religions." Unitarian Universalist Church, Oak Ridge, TN. 15-17 March 2002.

Lund, David H. *Death and Consciousness*. Jefferson, NC: McFarland, 1985.

Man Ho, Kwok, et al. *The Fortune-Teller's I-Ching: A Completely New Translation of the Most Famous Oracle in the World*. London: Rider, 1986.

Masterson, James F., M.D. *The Real Self: A Developmental, Self, and Object Relations Approach*. New York: Bruner-Mazel, 1985.

Mathews, Robert C., and Rena D. Mister. "Measuring an Individual's Investment in the Future: Symbolic Immortality, Sensation Seeking, and Psychic Numbness." *Omega: Journal of Death and Dying*. Robert J. Kastenbaum, Ph.D., ed. Farmingdale, NY: Baywood. 18.3 (1987-88).

McCarthy, James B. *Death Anxiety: The Loss of the Self*. New York: Gardner, 1980.

McCoy, Marjorie Casebier. *To Die with Style!* Nashville: Abingdon, 1974.

Miller, Alice. *The Drama of the Gifted Child: The Search for the True Self*. Rev. Ed. New York: Basic Books, 1994.

Mills, Gretchen, et al. *Discussing Death: A Guide to Death Education*. Homewood, IL: ETC, 1976.

Mor, Vincent, Ph.D., David S. Greer, M.D., and Robert J. Kastenbaum, Ph.D. *The Hospice Experiment*. Baltimore: Johns Hopkins University Press, 1988.

Morse, Melvin, M.D., with Paul Perry. *Closer to the Light: Learning from Children's Near-Death Experiences*. Foreword by Raymond A. Moody, M.D. New York: Villard, 1990.

Mullin, Glenn H. *Death and Dying: The Tibetan Tradition*. Boston: Arkana, 1986.

Munnicks, J.M.A. *Old Age and Finitude*. Basel: S. Karger, 1966.

Mylonas, George. *Eleusis and the Eleusinian Mysteries*. Princeton: Princeton University Press, 1961.

Nhât Hanh, Thich. *The Sun My Heart*. Berkeley: Parallax, 1988.

Nuland, Sherwin. *How We Die*. New York: Knopf, 1994.

O'Kill, Brian. *Exit Lines: Famous (and not-so-famous) Last Words*. Essex, England: Longman, 1986.

Osbon, Diane K., ed. *A Joseph Campbell Companion: Reflections on the Art of Living*. New York: Harper-Collins, 1991.

Panati, Charles. *Panati's Extraordinary Endings of Practically Everything and Everyone*. New York: Harper & Row, 1989.

PBS Home Video. *American Experience: Seabiscuit*. Boston: WGBH-TV, 2003.

Pegg, Patricia F. and Erno Metze, eds. *Death and Dying: A Quality of Life.* Bath: Pitman, 1981.
Primavesi, Anne. *Gaia's Gift: Earth, Ourselves, and God After Copernicus.* London: Routledge, 2003.
—. *Making God Laugh: Human Arrogance and Ecological Humility.* Santa Rosa, CA: Polebridge Press, 2004.
Rosenthal, Ted. *How Could I Not Be Among You?* New York: George Braziller, 1973.
Roslansky, John D. Discussion. "The End of Life." Nobel Conference, 1972. Amsterdam: North-Holland, 1973.
Rowe, Dorothy. *The Construction of Life and Death.* Chichester: John Wiley, 1982.
Saunders, Cicely, Dame. "Spiritual Pain." *Hospital Chaplain.* St. Christopher's Fourth International Conference. March 1988.
Schultz, Richard, and David Aderman. "Physicians' Death Anxiety and Patient Outcomes." *Omega: Journal of Death and Dying.* Robert J. Kastenbaum, Ph.D., ed. Farmingdale, NY: Baywood. 9.4 (1978-79).
—. And Janet Schlarb. "Two Decades of Research on Dying: What Do We Know About the Patient?" *Omega: Journal of Death and Dying.* Robert J. Kastenbaum, Ph.D., ed. Farmingdale, NY: Baywood. 18.4 (1987-88).
Schweitzer, Albert. *Memories of Childhood and Youth.* New York: Macmillan, 1955.
Scott, Nathan, Jr., ed. *The Modern Vision of Death.* Richmond: John Knox, 1967.
Shneidman, Edwin. *Deaths of Man.* New York: Quadrangle/The New York Times Book Co., 1973.
—. *Definition of Suicide.* New York: Wiley, 1985.
—. *Voices of Death.* New York: Harper & Row, 1980.
Shroder, Tom. *Old Souls: The Scientific Evidence for Past Lives.* New York: Fireside/Simon & Schuster, 2001.
Simonton, O. Carl, M.D., Stephanie Mathews-Simonton, and James Creighton. *Getting Well Again: A Step-by-Step Self-Help Guide.* Los Angeles: Tarcher, 1978.
Simmons, Philip. *Learning to Fall: The Blessings of an Imperfect Life.* New York: Bantam, 2003.
Skinner, Cornelia Otis. *Madame Sarah.* Boston: Houghton-Mifflin, 1966.
Smyth, Joshua M., and James W. Pennebaker. "Sharing One's Story: Translating Emotional Experiences into Words as a Coping Tool." *Coping: The Psychology of What Works.* C. R. Snyder, ed. New York & Oxford: Oxford University Press, 1999.

Solomon, Deborah. "Taking Religious Liberties." *The New York Times.* 4 April 2004.

Spiro, Howard M., Mary G. McCrea Curnen and Lee Palmer Wandel, eds. *Facing Death: Where Culture, Religion, and Medicine Meet.* New Haven & London: Yale University Press, 1996.

Spong, John Shelby. Lecture. Westar Institute Millennium Symposium. Santa Rosa, CA. February 2000.

Stern, Paul. *C. G. Jung: The Haunted Prophet.* New York: George Braziller, 1976.

Taylor, Jean H., and Norman K. Perrill. "The Hospice Environmental Survey (HES): Pilot Test of a New Measurement Instrument." *Omega: Journal of Death and Dying.* Robert J. Kastenbaum, Ph.D., ed. Farmingdale, NY: Baywood. 18.3 (1987-88).

Taylor, Jeremy. *The Rule and Exercises of Holy Dying.* London: Richard Royston, 1651.

Tolstoy, Leo. *Confessions.* (1882). London: Oxford, 1961.

—. *Short Novels: Volume Two.* Introduction by Ernest J. Simmons. New York: Modern Library, 1966.

Toynbee, Arnold. "Changing Attitudes Toward Death in the Modern Western World." *Man's Concern with Death.* Arnold Toynbee, et al. New York: McGraw-Hill, 1969.

Twycross, Robert, Dr., and Dr. Sylvia Lack. *Oral Morphine.* Beaconsfield Bucks, England: Beaconsfield, 1988.

Ulin, Richard O. *Death and Dying Education.* Washington, D.C.: National Education Association, 1977.

USA Today-CNN-Gallup. Poll, December 1999. As cited in *Religion Today.* 29 December 1999.

Valpy, Michael. "God is Big These Days." *Shambhala Sun.* January 2005, pp. 38-41.

Van Tassel, David D., ed. *Aging, Death, and the Completion of Being.* Philadelphia: University of Pennsylvania Press, 1979.

Walker, Kenneth. *The Circle of Life: A Search for an Attitude to Pain, Disease, Old Age, and Death.* College Park, MD: McGrath, 1970.

Wallach, Janet. *Desert Queen: The Extraordinary Life of Gertrude Bell— Adventurer, Adviser to Kings, Ally of Lawrence of Arabia.* (1996). New York: Anchor Books Ed., 1999.

Wehr, Gerhard. *Jung: A Biography.* Boston: Shambhala, 1987.

Weisman, Avery D., M.D. *The Coping Capacity: On the Nature of Being Mortal.* New York: Human Sciences Press, 1984.

Wells, Robert V. *Facing the "King of Terrors": Death and Society in an American Community, 1750-1990.* Cambridge: Cambridge University Press, 2000.

Wholey, Dennis. *Are You Happy?* Boston: Houghton-Mifflin, 1986.

Wuthnow, Robert. *Creative Spirituality: The Way of the Artist.* Berkeley, Los Angeles, London: University of California Press, 2001.

INDEX

Addison, Joseph, post-self immortality—37
Advanced Directives, Living Will—128
African-Americans, death rituals—92
Afterlife belief—8, 75, 109, 138, 152, 176, 198
    Cons—133
    Pros—150
AIDS—89, 114, 118
Alaskan Indians, study, Trelease, Murray—128
Allen, Woody, themes in movies—46, 63, 99
American individualism, ego—16, 27, 32, 38, 48, 59, 62, 67, 73, 81, 176, 188
American "way to go," afterlife, family support—152
"And the Music is You"—24
Aries, Philippe, attitudes toward death—86, 89, 134
Armstrong, Karen—18, 71, 78, 147, 171, 177, 188
    Ash Wednesday, T. S. Eliot—19
    Borg, Marcus, author, Armstrong colleague—18
    Finding her bliss—19, 59
    History of God, A—18
    Muhammad—79
    Personal role model—196
    Qur'an's inclusive spirit—153
    See, Carolyn, Armstrong reviewer—18
    The Spiral Staircase—18, 188
    Wordsworth mantra—97, 196
Atchley, Robert, *Social Forces of Aging*—152
Authentic life, real self—17, 19, 21, 25, 36, 40, 48, 59, 70, 73
Axial (Pivotal) Age wisdom—19, 194
Bacon, Francis, on fear of death—133
Barrett, Deirdre, study, death dreams—155
Baumeister, Roy F., *Meanings in Life*—63, 74
Becker, Ernest
    The Denial of Death—9, 12, 111, 150, 187
    Escape from Evil—134, 138
Beckett, Samuel, post-self immortality—32
Belief in heaven, hell—75, 109, 139, 141, 161, 166, 172
Belief in Big Mind, creed, deity —6, 19, 28, 35, 41, 71, 77, 81, 109, 134, 136, 141, 150

Bell, Gertrude—42
Bergman, Ingmar, *Wild Strawberries*, confronting death—22
Bernhardt, Sarah
    Churchill, Sir Winston, handling failure—97
    Esprit, flaws and all—95
    Personal role model for morale, spiritual first mate—95, 195
Besht, The, Baal Shem Tov—180
Big Mind—28, 71, 77, 79, 109, 188
BLAP (Badly Lucked And Patterned people)—57
"Blew It" anxiety—2, 6, 15, 24
Bliss—4, 15, 17, 19, 40, 58, 66, 68, 121, 124, 185
Book of Common Prayer, The—87
Borg, Marcus, author, Armstrong colleague—18
Boston, Sarah and Rachel Trezise, achieving the last goal—100
Boyle and Morriss, *The Mirror of Time*—40
Bremmer, Jan, *Rise and Fall of the Afterlife, The*—157, 161
British Society of Psychical Research, The—169
Britton and Bootzin, NDE and sleep—165
Buber, Martin, "I-thou" relationship—179
Buddha, Buddhism—19, 25, 27, 58, 70, 80, 104, 121, 137, 145, 156, 171, 182, 194
Budge, Sir Wallis, Egyptian ethics, death—153
Butler, Dr. Robert, *Why Survive?*—22, 33, 45, 69, 72
Byock, Dr. Ira, *Dying Well*—126, 129
Callahan, Daniel, transforming breakthrough—61
Campbell, Joseph—3, 7, 17, 20, 33, 40, 47, 58, 66, 177, 183, 188, 194
Camus, Albert, *Myth of Sysiphus, The*, search for fulfillment—64
Capra, Frank, death and rebirth in films, our effect on others—39, 169
Carey, Raymond, study, fears at time of death—115, 117
Cataloguing, rare books, *otherwise fine*—4
Children, teenagers—16, 48, 92, 163
    Childhood dreams—1, 3
    Parental, societal influences—16, 48, 51
    Psychic Phenomena—163, 166, 170
    Suicide--106
Cicero, *De Legibus*, Eleusinian Mysteries—133
Clarke-Howes, Dr. Nicholas—169
Climber, letting go—13, 85, 87, 133, 195
Cohen, Dr. Gene, *The Creative Age*—28
Compassion—70, 78, 80, 194, 197
Completeness, potential fulfilled—16, 26, 30, 42, 52, 59, 63, 68, 185, 188
Confucius—19, 23, 70, 143

Cons, afterlife belief—8, 133
  Believer vs. nonbeliever—138
  Gaia theory—136
  Geography of heaven, hell—109, 139
  Jesus, atonement—140
  Judgment vs. reincarnation—140
  Karma and the untouchables—139
  Martyrs of Cordova—146
  Mithraism and Christianity—144
  Parable vs. reality—145
  Sacrifices for salvation—139
Conscience—70, 73, 78
Coping—8, 11, 25, 28, 36, 59, 103, 106, 195
  Bernhardt, Sarah—95
  Choice, creativity—35, 59, 105
  Churchill, Sir Winston—97
  Exercises, patterns, strategies—21, 104, 110, 183
    Course in Miracles, A—104
    Rutters—99, 124, 194
    Stevenson, Robert Louis—97
  Potential, purpose, perspective—27, 58, 62, 68, 75, 80, 185
Cross-correspondence, medium, channeling—159
Cupitt, Don, solar living/ethics—79, 185
D-Day (Death Day) exercise—21, 24, 77, 124
  Completion Days—21
Darwin, Charles, immortality—77, 111
Death and rebirth—19, 22, 26, 28, 33, 39, 77, 79, 133, 153, 169, 184
Death anxiety
  "Alcoholics and Death Anxiety"—2
  Heightened—2, 5, 8, 48, 57, 64, 68, 73, 85, 114, 122, 126
  Lowered—1, 6, 8, 11, 26, 34, 36, 62, 65, 69, 73, 79, 89, 103, 106, 108, 110, 114
  Medicine and technology—86, 125
  Physical process
    dependency, prolonged illness—16, 49, 52, 88, 114, 117
    losing one's looks—49
    loss of control, dignity—16, 49, 86, 126, 184
    pain—16, 49, 114, 124, 125
  Regarding those left behind—88, 115, 122
  Separation, solitude—8, 16, 27, 32, 48, 51, 63, 65, 88, 115, 123
  Support—8, 37, 86, 119
  Variables—9, 86, 122
  "Worm"—5, 6, 12, 57, 148

Death of Ellen Augusta—151
Dee, John, psychomanteum—158
Dreams
    Adult—1, 7
    Childhood—1, 3
    Relation to Near-Death Experience—155, 163
Dying alone—123
Eckhart, Meister, mystic—181
Edelen, William, mystical intuition—181
Ego, individualism—16, 27, 32, 36, 38, 48, 59, 62, 67, 69, 73, 81, 176, 188
Eqyptians, ancient, ethics, immortality—32, 121, 153
Einstein, Albert—176, 181
Eleusinian Mysteries—133, 161
Elias, Norbert, attitudes toward death—87
Eliot, T. S., *Ash Wednesday*—19
entelechy, defined—15
Epicureans—184
Ethical wills—38
Exclusive identity—150
Exercises
    D-Day (Death Day)—21, 24, 77, 124
    Life review—22, 45, 77
    Meditation—19, 154, 183
    Thanatopics: Activities and Exercises for Confronting Death—24
Facing Death, Robert E. Kavanaugh—7
Faith—78, 90, 189
Fears of death
    "Blew It" anxiety—2, 6, 15, 24
    Childhood—1, 3, 16, 92, 106
    Extinction with insignificance—8, 16, 32, 76, 176
    Failure and anger—18, 27
    Inauthentic life—3, 8, 19, 28, 62, 73, 77
    Judgment—8, 16, 23, 32, 35, 59, 114
    Loss of self
        American individualism, ego—16, 27, 32, 36, 38, 48, 59, 62, 67, 69, 73, 81, 176, 188
        immortality—32, 35, 55, 60, 63, 75, 114
        suicide—99, 100, 106
    Miller, Alice, *The Drama of the Gifted Child*—49
    Nothingness, non-existence, the unknown—8, 15
    Psychological needs—7, 9, 17, 26, 58, 69, 103
        Bergman, Ingmar, *Wild Strawberries*—22

Simonton, Carl and Stephanie-Matthews-Simonton, *Getting Well Again*—22
   Relationship to religiosity—18, 23, 73, 150
   Unmet potential, incompleteness—11, 15, 23, 25, 28, 42, 52, 55, 62, 67, 77, 176
   late- and never-bloomers—28, 45, 48, 55, 67
   premature death—16, 24, 26, 32
Feifel, Herman, medicine and technology—88
False, forced, impaired identities—46, 73, 169
Frame and death—73
   Hindu, "kicking the frame"—5
   Japan, drawing ends outside the frame—5, 77
Frankl, Viktor, family support—120
Friedman, Alan, "Death as a Cultural Phenomenon,"—86, 89
Freud, Sigmund, coping strategies—110
Functioned out, no quality of life—118
Gaia
   gifts—137, 186
   theory, by James Lovelock—137
Garrett, Eileen, medium, author, psychic—159
   R101, British dirigible—160
Goldberg, Ivan, pain relief—125
Goodman, Dr. Lisl, creativity, death fears—16, 32, 36, 59, 154
   D-Day (Death Day) exercise—21, 24, 77, 124
   Death and the Creative Life—15
Gorer, Geoffrey, *Death, Grief, and Mourning*—85
Grant, Ulysses S., morale—107
Greyson, Dr. C. Bruce, coping patterns—165
Hailey, Oliver, *For the Use of the Hall*, creative failure—37
Harris, Jill, attitudes toward death—90
Heidegger, Martin, German philosopher, thanatologist—12
Hillel and the Torah—142
Hillenbrand, Laura, *Seabiscuit*—55
Hindu (*See also* India.)
   "Kicking the frame"—5
Hitchcock, Alfred, identity themes in movies—46, 68
Hodgson, Marshall G.S., *The Venture of Islam*, respect—78
Holmes, Oliver Wendall, Jr., outside the frame—5
Holy Grail—188
Hopi Indian, death and rebirth—40
Hospice—6, 8, 87, 114
   Goals—115

Oral histories—106
Respect for the dying, 128
Saunders, Dame Cecily, St. Christopher's Hospice—88, 114, 128, 179
Humor—57, 96, 108
Huxley, Aldous, *Doors of Perception,* "Mind at Large,"—155
Imhof, Arthur, *ars moriendi,* dying right—124
Incompleteness, unmet potential—11, 15, 23, 28, 32, 42, 45, 48, 52, 55, 62, 67, 77, 176
India (*See also* Hindu.)
    Death—5, 121
    Gandhi, Caste system of India, the untouchables—139, 156
    Karma—139
    Krishna, nonpartisan belief—142
    Reincarnation—76, 139, 156, 166
    Shakti, divine energy—186
Individualism, ego—16, 27, 32, 38, 48, 59, 62, 67, 73, 81, 176, 188
Irish, Donald P., death rituals—91
Islam—18, 109
    Muhammad, societal issues—141, 147, 196
    Qur'an, Holy Book of Islam—121, 141, 153, 196
    Sufis—153
James, William, "worm at the core"—5, 12, 26, 77, 79, 95, 148, 173
Japan
    Drawing ending outside the frame—5, 77
    Lifton, Robert Jay, study, immortality—34
    Suicide, *hara kiri, seppuku*—101
Jesus—70, 137, 139, 140, 143, 153, 196
Jews, Judaism—18, 70
    Afterlife beliefs—110
    Besht, The, holy sparks—180
    Hillel and the Torah—142
    Holocaust—143, 150
    Mystics, psychic phenomena—162, 180
    Respect for the dying—128
Jung, Carl—42, 65, 110, 136, 187, 198
Kalish, Richard, attitude toward death—88, 153
Kastenbaum, Robert J., Ph.D.—2, 8, 64
    Belief systems—90, 139, 156
    Is There Life After Death?—157
    Morale and humor—108
    On Our Way, death ritual—90
    Psychic phenomena—157

Reincarnation—168
Kastenbaum, Robert J., Ph.D., and Beatrice Kastenbaum, National Hospice Demonstration Study—115
Kavanaugh, Robert E., *Facing Death*—7, 78, 110, 138, 184
Kearl, Michael
    Afterlife belief—75
    Study, losing one's looks—49
"Kicking the frame"—5
Krauss, Rabbi, climber, letting go—13
Krishna, nonpartisan believers—142
Kubler-Ross, Dr. Elisabeth—26, 83, 88, 119
    Five stages of reactions to death—102
Lakota Indians, afterlife—91
Lao-Tzu—19, 81
Lapidus, Ira, Muslim at death—121
Late- and never-bloomers—28, 45, 55, 99
    "Carpenter, Larry"—29, 52
    Edmonson, William—28
Lee, Dr. Elizabeth, *In Your Own Time*, relief with drugs—125
Lee, Sander, identity themes in movies—46
Leming Death Fear Scale—114
Lennon, John, *Imagine*—148
Lerner, Alan Jay, purpose in life—37
Letting go—8, 13, 26, 70, 85, 93, 118, 124, 129, 187
    American "way to go"—152
    How to—27, 77, 122
    Preparing for death—11, 17, 74, 85, 92
    Toynbee, Arnold—92
    With significance—129
Lifton, Robert Jay
    Immortality symbols—169
    Post-self modes—33
        genes—33, 38
        memory held by others—33, 39
        special mode of experiential transcendence—33, 39
        theological and natural—33, 40
        transplant into the body of others—33
        works—33, 36, 38, 110
    Study, Chinese, Japanese, on immortality—34
Loehr, Reverend Davidson, Christianity and Mithraism—144
Lovelock, James, Gaia theory—137
Luck, patterns—56
    BLAP (Badly Lucked And Patterned people)—57

Lund, David, brain after death—154
Luther, Martin—20, 73
Main Four, The—119
Maintaining boundaries
    Purpose in life—58, 62, 68, 77, 185
    Self-esteem—3, 23, 25, 28, 30, 49, 57, 59, 64, 67, 73, 77, 183
Malraux, Andre, *La Condition Humaine*—64
Martyrs of Cordova, Perfectus—146
Masterson, James, *The Real Self*—46
Mathews and Mister, study, immortality—34
McCarthy, James
    Finding purpose and identity—62
    Separation conflicts—48
Medicine and technology—86, 125
    Confusion—127
    Depression, sleeplessness—126
Mediumship, or channeling—160, 170
Mexican-Americans, death rituals—92
Miller, Alice
    Lack of mirroring in childhood—49
    Losing one's looks—49
Morale—106, 116
Montaigne, Michel de—12, 192
Moody, Dr. Raymond, Jr., psychomanteum—158
Moving outside the frame—5, 73, 77, 81, 189
    Death and rebirth—19, 22, 33, 169
Moyers, Bill, *Power of Myth*—177
Muhammad, enlightened ecumenism—141, 147, 197
Muslim, recite Qur'an at deathbed—121
Myers, F.W.H., a founder, British Society of Psychical Research, The—158
    Cross-correspondence—159
Mysticism—179
    Besht, The—180
    Eckhart, Meister—181
    Edelen, William—181
    Einstein, Albert—181
    Gnostic Gospel of Thomas—137, 180
    Goodenough, Ursula—182
    Gospel of Thomas—180
    Sufism—180
Myth Indicators
    Adult dreams—3
    Childhood dreams—1, 3, 40

Death and rebirth—19, 23, 40, 169
   In Joseph Campbell's life—3, 7, 40
   Transforming breakthrough—3, 19, 61
Native Americans
   Alaskan Indians, control at death—128
   Apache, empty body—90
   Death and rebirth—40, 90
   Hopi Indians, rebirth—40
   Irish, Donald P.—90
   Lakota, Dr. Martin Brokenleg—91
   Navajo, no afterlife—91
   Pueblo Indians, afterlife—40
   Symbols and rituals—89
Near-Death Experience (NDE)— 155, 163, 165
Negative Golden Rule, The—21
New Zealanders, afterlife belief—75, 90
Nhât Hanh, Thich, *The Sun My Heart*—137
Nobel, Alfred, prize endowment—38
Noble, Dr. Ernest, UCLA Alcohol Research Center—52
Nuland, Dr. Sherwin
   Near-Death Experience—163
   Violent or catastrophic trauma—105
Out-of-Body Experience (OBE)—161, 164
   Sabom, Dr. Michael, cardiologist—164
"Outside the frame"—6, 189
Partridge, Dr. Linda, "Low-Calorie-Diet Study Takes Scientists Aback"—60
Pollard, Red, *Seabiscuit*—55, 60
Polls
   Gallup Organization—109
   General Social Surveys—75
   Harris Poll—171
   International Social Survey Program—75
   Leming Death Fear Scale—114
   Survey Research Center, UC/Berkeley—110
   USA Today-CNN-Gallup—110
Ponet, James—30
Post-self—32
   Bell, Gertrude—42
   Modes, Lifton, Robert Jay—33
      genes—33, 38
      memory held by others—33, 38
      special mode of experiential transcendence—33, 39
      theological and natural—33, 40, 42, 110

    transplant into the body of others—33
    works, business—33, 38
        Barnum, P. T., promoter—38
        Nobel, Alfred, prize endowment—38
    works, creative—33, 36, 110
        Goodman, Lisl—36
        Hailey, play—37
        Tolstoy, Leo, characters—36
    Native Americans—40
    Study, immortality, Chinese, Japanese—34
    Study, immortality, Mathews and Mister—34
Prematurely dying—15, 21, 24, 32
Preparing for death
    Afterlife belief—8, 77, 109, 138, 152, 176, 198
    Authentic self—17, 19, 21, 25, 36, 40, 48, 59, 70, 73
    Commitment to creed, others, self—34, 46, 69, 73, 77, 108
    Coping mechanisms—8, 11, 28, 36, 48, 59, 62, 88, 99, 106, 183
        change in perspective—58, 66, 77, 81
        morale—106, 116
        rutters—99, 124, 194
    Dreams—155
    Exercises
        D-Day (Death Day)— 21, 24, 77, 124
        life review—22, 46, 124
        meditation—19, 104, 183
    Family, hospice, relationship—87, 106, 114, 120
    Medicine and technology—86, 125
    Near-Death Experience—155, 163, 165
    Recognizing potential, self-fulfillment—15, 25, 56, 62, 74
    Symbols and rituals—89, 106, 116, 119
Primavesi, Dr. Anne
    Ecology vs. humanity—136
    Gaia theory, by James Lovelock—137
    Gaia's Gift—136
    Making God Laugh—136
Pros, afterlife belief—8
    Appreciation of other religions, Sufis, Islam—153
    Conduct determines destiny, Egypt—152
    Conquer. lose one's ego—154, 189, 198
    Consciousness transmissions—155
    Near-Death, Out-of-Body Experiences—155, 165
    Psychic phenomena—157
    Reincarnation, positive humanitarian effects—157, 165

Study, dreams show positive hope—155
Survival with "Mind at Large"—155
Process of dying—8, 15
    Dependency—16, 51, 88, 111, 114, 127
    Loss of control, dignity—16, 49, 86, 126, 184
    Pain—16, 49, 114, 124, 125
    Solitude—8, 16, 27, 32, 47, 51, 63, 65, 88, 115, 119, 123
Pueblo Indians, death and rebirth, pit houses—40
Psychic phenomena—8, 156, 178
    Astrology, I Ching—172
    Clarke-Howes, Dr. Nicholas—169
    Death-bed escort—160
    Is There Life After Death?, Robert J. Kastenbaum—157
    Medium, or channeling—159, 161, 165, 170
    "Mind at Large," access to all knowledge—155
    Mysticism—65, 179
    Near-Death Experience (NDE)—156, 162
        Greyson, Dr. C. Bruce—165
        study, Britton and Bootzin—165
    Necromancy—162
    Out-of-Body Experience (OBE)—158, 161, 164, 168
        Sabom, Dr. Michael, cardiologist—164
    Pluralistic death—165, 168
    Poltergeists, or ghosts—158, 170
    Psychomanteum—158, 160
    Reincarnation—156, 161, 165, 171
    Rise and Fall of the Afterlife, The, Jan Bremmer—157, 161
    Stevenson, Dr. Ian—165
Pythagoreans, Orphism—161
Rank, Otto, creativity, immortality—36, 66
Real self
    Authentic self—17, 19, 21, 25, 36, 40, 48, 59, 70, 73
    Identity—5, 41, 48, 62, 65, 71, 85, 167
    Personal belief system—46, 73
    Purpose in life—38, 63, 68, 77
    Self-esteem—3, 23, 25, 28, 30, 49, 57, 59, 64, 67, 73, 77, 183
Release of Judgment—187
Relationship
    Doctor-patient—119, 122
    Minister and family—122
Religiosity
    Big Mind—28, 71, 77, 79, 109, 188
    Christian vs. non-Christian—118, 138, 189

Cultural differences—64, 70, 109, 140, 150
Death and rebirth—19, 22, 26, 28, 33, 39, 77, 79, 133, 153, 169, 184
Faith, commitment—73, 78, 109, 140, 189
Relieves fear of death—8, 75, 110, 118
Theology of—2, 8, 70
Retirement community, alone—122
Role models, personal
    Armstrong, Karen—196
    Bernhardt, Sarah—195
Rosenthal, Ted, incompleteness—15, 22, 24, 26, 62, 115
Rule and Exercises of Holy Dying, The, Taylor, Jeremy—11, 122, 187
    "The Epistle Dedicatory"—11
Rutters, coping mechanisms—8, 99, 123, 194
Saunders, Dame Cecily, Britain, St. Christopher's Hospice—88, 114, 179
Schultz, Richard and Janet Schlarb, study, patient deaths—119
Schweitzer, Albert, our effect on others—69
Scott, Nathan, *The Modern Vision of Death*—12
Seabiscuit—55
See, Carolyn, Armstrong reviewer—18
Self-esteem—3, 23, 25, 28, 30, 49, 57, 59, 64, 67, 73, 77, 183
Selwyn, Dr. Peter, doctor-patient relationship—119
September 11, 2001—150, 177
Shneidman, Edwin—32, 33, 45, 73
    Categories of death
        appropriate—100
        partial—101
        psychological—101
        significant—101
        unintentioned, intentioned, subintentioned—101
    Coping skills—103
    Dying prematurely—21
    Personal belief system—73
    Post-self—32
        memory held by others—32
        natural mode, Japanese students—34
    Suicide, *Voices of Death*—99, 106, 157
    Survey, *Psychology Today*—87
Sikhism, monotheistic religion—109
Simmons, Philip—26, 71, 79
    Learning to Fall—26
    Letting go—26
Simonton, Carl and Stephanie-Matthews-Simonton

Death and rebirth, life review—22, 25
   Getting Well Again—22
Smith, Tom, *Seabiscuit*—55
Smythe, Joshua and James, Pennebaker, coping strategies—106
Socrates, Axial (Pivotal) Age wisdom—19
Solar living, solar ethics, Don Cupitt—79, 185
Spirituality, faith—178
   Concepts as linchpin—178
   "Divine Mystery, The"—179, 181
   Meditation—103, 124, 183
      as reading—183
   Mysticism—180
   Of empathy, Holy Grail—188
   Of Gaia—186
   Of the offering—187
   Of outwardness, solar living—185
   Of personal sacred spaces—179
   Spiritual humanism—184
   Twelve-Step Program—184
   Unifying force—179
Spong, Bishop John Shelby, ascent vs. orbit—109, 140
Statistics—8, 51, 75, 87, 88, 92, 114, 119, 125, 139, 150, 170, 172
Stevenson, Dr. Ian, reincarnation—165, 173
   Birth- or other marks—167
   Previous knowledge—168
   Shroder, Tom, traveling with Stevenson—166
   Xenoglossy—167
Studies—2, 8, 34, 49, 52, 59, 62, 69, 86, 115, 116, 119, 125, 128, 152, 155, 158, 164
Substance abusers
   A1 allele in DRD2 gene—53
   "Alcoholics and Death Anxiety"—2
   Chemical imbalances—53
   Early-onset alcoholic—51, 54
   Geriatric alcoholism—52
   Morphine and opioids, pain relief—125
   Study, Dr. Ernest Noble—52
   Treatment—29, 53, 125
Sufism, Islam
   Al-Bistami, mystics—153, 180
   Appreciation of other religions—153, 180
   Rumi, poet, writer of Sufi scripture—154
Suicide

    Allen, Woody—99
    Japanese *hara kiri, seppuku*—101
    Loss of self—99
    Mayans—101
    Rutters—99, 124, 194
    Shneidman, Dr. Edwin, suicidology—99
    Teen—106
Survival essentials—204
Symbols and rituals—89
Taylor, Jeremy
    Rule and Exercises of Holy Dying, The, "The Epistle Dedicatory"—11, 187
    "The Manner of Visitation"—122
Thanatopics: Activities and Exercises for Confronting Death—24
Thomas, Helen, controlling choices—68
Tillich, Paul, the courage to be—65
Tolstoy, Leo, attitudes toward death—23, 36, 93
Toynbee, Arnold—92
Trelease, Murray, study, Alaskan Indians, control at death—128
Twelve-Step Program—134, 184
Unamuno, Miguel, post-self immortality—35
Unmet potential, incompleteness—11, 15, 23, 28, 32, 42, 45, 48, 52, 55, 62, 67, 77, 176
Wallach, Janet, *Desert Queen*, biography of Gertrude Bell—42
Watson, James, no afterlife belief—35
Weinberg, Stephen, damage religion does—181
Weisman, Dr. Avery, coping strategies—100, 107
Wells, Robert, *Facing the "King of Terrors"*—86
Wigner, Eugene Paul, no desire to return—154
Wild Strawberries, Ingmar Bergman, confronting death—22
Woodcuts, learning to die—123
"Worm at the core"—5, 12, 57, 110, 148
Wuthnow, Robert, spirituality—179
Xenoglossy—167

About the Author

Susan Barry was the originator and first Administrative Director of the Rice University Publishing Program. Later pertinent freelance credits included regional book promotion for New York publishing houses, newspaper book reviews, and writing credits that extend broadly from a WABC-TV scriptwriting award for creative programming to a children's play which was placed in the National Archives. She has researched, written and edited for a rare book house, an experience to which the title of this book is indebted. Hospice-related, she produced a training video for caregivers for the Hospice at the Texas Medical Center and has been both a professional and volunteer member of a hospice team. This is her first book and special legacy to Drew and Brice.